# The Year of the Poet VIII

## June 2021

**The Poetry Posse**

inner child press, ltd.

# The Poetry Posse 2021

Gail Weston Shazor
Shareef Abdur Rasheed
Teresa E. Gallion
hülya n. yılmaz
Kimberly Burnham
Tzemin Ition Tsai
Elizabeth Esguerra Castillo
Jackie Davis Allen
Joe Paire
Caroline 'Ceri' Nazareno
Ashok K. Bhargava
Alicja Maria Kuberska
Swapna Behera
Albert 'Infinite' Carrasco
Eliza Segiet
William S. Peters, Sr.

In order to maintain each poet's authentic voice, this volume has not undergone the scrutiny of editing. Please take time to indulge each contributor for their own creativity and aspirations to convey their uniqueness.

hülya n. yılmaz, Ph.D.
Director of Editing ~
Inner Child Press International

# General Information

## The Year of the Poet VIII

**June 2021 Edition**

## The Poetry Posse

**1st Edition : 2021**



**Publisher Information**

**1st Edition : Inner Child Press**
**intouch@innerchildpress.com**
**www.innerchildpress.com**



ISBN-13 : 978-1-952081-50-7 (inner child press, ltd.)

$ 12.99

WHAT WOULD

LIFE

BE WITHOUT

A LITTLE

POETRY?

# Dedication

This Book is dedicated to

*Humanity, Peace & Poetry*

the Power of the Pen

can effectuate change!

&

The Poetry Posse

past, present & future

our Patrons and Readers

the Spirit of our Everlasting Muse

*In the darkness of my life*
*I heard the music*
*I danced . . .*
*and the Light appeared*
*and I dance*

Janet P. Caldwell

# Table of Contents



## The Poetry Posse

## Table of Contents . . . *continued*

# Foreword

June marks the halfway point for the year. It says to us “you have been successful thus far”. Rayen Kang lives this as a young artist. The laurels of her early success will not rest here. The vision of conservation by young people can only be surpassed by the continued work.

There is no where one can turn without seeing information on climate change. What happened, what it is and how we need to change our lives is on the top of the list from the office of the President down to the youngest citizen. Rayen supports this through her art. Her “voice” brings awareness to the issues important to her. The realism in her choices of fowl bring us into her reality. We may only see a duck or a swan but the 80 plus hours she spent getting it true to her eye shows in how we appreciate the canvas.

The world has yet to weigh in on this young lady. She, however, is busy weighing in on the world. Helping out as a research assistant on quantile estimation, presiding over the STEAM organization at Georgia Tech, and spending time encouraging other young women in the STEM field, she is making marks in tackling real world problems in a challenging environment.

In this issue of the Year of the Poet, you will be challenged to see how we acknowledge the contributions of youth and how we see ourselves at the turning point of the year. We may allow our pens to reminiscence or dream forward. A very special thanks to the contributing poets. Keep in mind that you may think to yourself, “that is that piece”, there is always more to come. The art cannot be stilled.

Gail Weston Shazor
Director of Anthologies

# Preface

Dear Family and Friends,

So, here we are, ½ way through our eighth year of monthly publication of *The Year of the Poet*. Amazing how much effort has been given by all the poets, to include the various members of *The Poetry Posse* and all the wonderful featured poets from all over our world. For myself, it has been and continues to be a great honor to be a part of this wonderful cooperative effort.

Last year, 2020 has been challenging for many of us throughout the year. We at *Inner Child Press International* were busy. We envisioned our role where the arts meet humanity to continue doing what we were good at . . . publishing. We managed to not only produce and publish this series, *The Year of the Poet* each month, but we were also very proactive in the arena of human and social consciousness. We were able to produce several other anthologies to include: World Healing, World Peace 2020; CORONA . . . social distancing; The Heart of a Poet; W.A.R. . . we are revolution; Poetry, the Best of 2020. Going forward, we are seeking to invest in the same or greater effort towards contributing to a 'conscious humanity'. We, poets and writers do have something to say about it all, and we intend to do so in any and every way we can. So stay tuned . . .

*Bill*

William S. Peters, Sr.

Publisher
Inner Child Press International

www.innerchildpress.com

*PS*

Do Not forget about the World Healing, World Peace Poetry initiative for 2022. Mark your calendars. Submissions will be opening . . .
**September 1st 2021**

Past volumes are vailable here

www.worldhealingworldpeacepoetry.com

**For Free Downloads of Previous Issues of The Year of the Poet**

www.innerchildpress.com/the-year-of-the-poet

# Rayen Kang

## June 2021

Rayen Kang, a 17 artist won the junior duck stamp contest. From Johns Creek, Georgia, Kang's Emperor goose artwork appears on the 2020 U.S. Postal Services' Duck stamp. The Junior Duck Stamp contest was created by the U.S. Fish and Wildlife Service to applaud conservation efforts by young people and support environmental and conservation education programs in the United States.

https://www.fws.gov/birds/education/junior-duck-stamp-conservation-program/junior-duck-stamp-gallery-2018-2019.php

"The Junior Duck Stamp Contest taught Rayen Kang over the years that however amazing paintings may be, they cannot compare to the wonders of real waterfowl, fueling her support for the conservation program."

2021-2022 South Carolina Junior Duck Stamp winner: "The King Has Arrived" by Julia Boyer Age 14, Charleston County School of the Arts, N. Charleston, SC

www.sewe.com/blog/2021-junior-duck-stamp/

Poets . . .
sowing seeds in the
Conscious Garden of Life,
that those who have yet to come
may enjoy the Flowers.

Poets, Writers . . . know that we are the enchanting magicians that nourishes the seeds of dreams and thoughts . . . it is our words that entice the hearts and minds of others to believe there is something grand about the possibilities that life has to offer and our words tease it forth into action . . . for you are the Poet, the Writer to whom the Gift of Words has been entrusted . . .

~ wsp

poetry is . . .
India INK

*Poetry succeeds where instruction fails.*

~ wsp

Gail
Weston
Shazor

This is a creative promise ~ my pen will speak to and for the world. Enamored with letters and respectful of their power, I have been writing for most of my life. A mother, daughter, sister and grandmother I give what I have been given, greatfilledly.

Author of . . .

"An Overstanding of an Imperfect Love"
&
Notes from the Blue Roof

Lies My Grandfathers Told Me

available at Inner Child Press.

www.facebook.com/gailwestonshazor
www.innerchildpress.com/gail-weston-shazor
navypoet1@gmail.com

# I imagine where your wings would have rested…

I imagine where your wings would have rested
Tickling for the birth
Downy pulsing under smooth flesh
The water gleams iridescently in rainbows
Arcing through the space of is and dreams

I imagine where your wings would have rested
In the two delicate spots cresting shoulder blades
Strongly erect and gently swaying
With a majesty of their own
And separate from the being you have become

I imagine where your wings would have rested
When they were hidden from view, from touch
I wonder if they felt pain or pleasure
When the water of your world
Has been contaminated with sludge

I imagine where your wings would have rested
Wanting to see the world as you do
Eager to be a part of your life for I imagined
Thoughts to be so much more interesting
Coming from your experiences in this nexttime

I imagine where your wings would have rested
I don't remember the tickle of gossamer feathers
Although it could have been mistaken
For the paint on canvas
Or the ink on a stamp

I imagine where your wings would have rested
Easy and peaceful
I imagine where my wings would have grown
Light and airy, filmy and fair
Had the world been as it was

# Dawtahs

I keep finding you
In the spaces that I
Forget to look
Some of you come to me
When I am done
And others when I need you
I have always been off step
A condition that I am used to
Having spent most
Of my life as one
Sometimes not
Sometimes so
But always mother wanted
And I promise that
I will always live you
Wrapped around my veins
So don't be afraid
To spread your arms open
For you have much to show me
And I have many more days
To share with you, this
The love of mothers
And the mothers before
And it will not leave you hungry
Nor subject to the falsehoods
Of this world
I want to share with you
A cradle legacy
Much more than breasts
And soft bellies, but
Of women nurturing women
Whether you want it or not
Come dawtah,
Let me love you into the brilliance
That is you

# Passing time

The old women smoke cigarettes
They roll them between arthritic
And yellowed fingers
Polished away of nicotine stains
Courtesy of now closed factories
And stockings with runs

The old women smoke cigarettes
Waving the smoke away from
The neighbor's noses
While telling their used to be stories
Of how they were once fancied
By prohibition runners in skinny pants

The old women smoke cigarettes
The viceroys and camels
Their long dead husbands favored
On the nights when it was too hot
Or too cold to keep warm on the corner
When called upon to light the stove

The old women smoke cigarettes
Passing them one to another
To light the next one's flame
The companionship in this one small act
Is enough to succor the widowhood
Of forgotten beautifulness

The old women smoke cigarettes
Because sometimes
One needs something to do with ones
Hands and mouths

# Alicja Maria Kuberska

Alicja Maria Kuberska – awarded Polish poetess, novelist, journalist, editor.

She is a member of the Polish Writers Associations in Warsaw, Poland and IWA Bogdani, Albania. She is also a member of directors' board of Soflay Literature Foundation, Our Poetry Archive (India) and Cultural Ambassador for Poland (Inner Child Press, USA )

Her poems have been published in numerous anthologies and magazines in : Poland, Czech Republic, Slovakia, Hungary,Ukraina, Belgium, Bulgaria, Albania, Spain, the UK, Italy, the USA, Canada, the UK, Argentina, Chile, Peru, Israel, Turkey, India, Uzbekistan, South Korea, Taiwan, China, Australia, South Africa, Zambia, Nigeria

She received two medals - the Nosside UNESCO Competition in Italy (2015) and European Academy of Science Arts and Letters in France (2017). Ahe also received a reward of international literary competition in Italy „ Tra le parole e 'elfinito" (2018). She was announced a poet of the 2017 year by Soflay Literature Foundation (2018).She also received : Bolesław Prus Prize Poland (2019), Culture Animator Poland (2019) and first prize Premio Internazionale di Poesia Poseidonia- Paestrum Italy (2019).

# Duck

A small bird crossed
 the calm surface of the lake.
The water rippled and wrinkled .

The charm of this moment
was reflected in the mirror of water.
The blue and white  feathers
 appeared in the green

This minute enchanted in postage stamps
still goes on and reminds of that time
as Mother Nature smiled
and sent colorful letters around the world

# A walk along the shores of the Baltic Sea

The sea breeze envelops me with nostalgia,
reverie rises in the air.

Screaming gulls like white sails
flutter on the endless ocean of the sky

I follow the calls of the birds
and I'm heading towards the distant horizon.

I leave footprints in the sand for a moment.
The waves sweep them away
with their arched arms .

Salty droplets fall on my face,
to flow meanders down my cheeks.

Water permeates my body and mind
and I want to know
the secrets of being and nothingness.

Nobody knows I've been here
and I'm becoming silence.
I disappear between the sea and the clouds.

## Other stars

Lights flashed in the sky,
as many as fireflies on a May night
- beautiful and dangerous.

Death stars
do not preach the good news.
They carry anger and regret.

Instead of angelic voices,
dawn and explosions,
moaning and crying can be heard.

Barbed wires around Bethlehem
hurt the land and the inhabitants
It does not allow wounds to heal.

Concrete stumps of houses
raise their destroyed hands to the sky
and mute lamentation and despair.

The stars exploded.
For the surrounding
towns and villages deadly debris fell.

Fire in the streets
are sparked by rebellion and anger.
Spring rain will not extinguish it.

Other stars bring destruction
- they reveal the truth
about peace that never existed.

Jackie
Davis
Allen

Jackie Davis Allen, otherwise known as Jacqueline D. Allen or Jackie Allen, grew up in the Cumberland Mountains of Appalachia. As the next eldest daughter of a coal miner father and a stay at home mother, she was the first in her family to attend and graduate from college. Her siblings, in their own right, are accomplished, though she is the only one, to date, that has discovered the gift of writing.

Graduating from Radford University, with a Bachelors of Science degree in Early Education, she taught in both public and private schools. For over a decade she taught private art classes to children both in her home and at a local Art and Framing Shop where she also sold her original soft sculptured Victorian dolls and original christening gowns.

She resides in northern Virginia with her husband, taking much needed get-aways to their mountain home near the Blue Ridge Mountains, a place that evokes memories of days spent growing up in the Appalachian Mountains.

A lover of hats, she has worn many. Following marriage to her college sweetheart, and as wife, mother, grandmother, teacher, tutor, artist, writer, poet and crafter, she is a lover of art and antiques, surrounding herself, always, with books, seeking to learn more.

In 2015 she authored *Looking for Rainbows, Poetry, Prose and Art*, and in 2017, *Dark Side of the Moon*. Both books of mostly narrative poetry were published by Inner Child Press and were edited by hulya n. yilmaz.

in 2019, No Illusions.Through the Looking Glass, which was nominated to be considered for a Pulitzer Prize by the publisher and editor of InnerChild Press, ltd.

http://www.innerchildpress.com/jackie-davis-allen.php
jackiedavisallen.com

# neyar gnak

quack, quack
duck stamp on the front
neyar gnak
image on the lake
paint me a scene
successful endeavor
an image impressed
like sticky rice in a bowl
a Chinese restaurant
Peking duck
simple things
complicated things
come to mind
think, smile; the title
an intellectual puzzle
not meant to offend
nor create a scene
simple intention
a note of levity

# A Vision of Truth

Buried in the annals of history,
Scrolls of truth waited. I held out my hand.
Traced it over the writings, the script strange.
Silent, it bade me to come in out of the dark.

Kneeling at the entrance to destiny,
I acquiesced. I discarded my mask.

I saw visions, saw dragons who breathed fire.
I saw rivers swallowing plumes of smoke.
I saw a chariot rise up on wings.

Herculean efforts to reach it failed.
Despite smoldering embers, I, like
Burnt offering, imbued with sweetest spice
Attracted a great crowd of truth's believers.

I sang songs, chanted prayers.
Like a mother bird on her nest, I held hope.

I nurtured the hope of a nation's desire;
Beseeched God that all might come into the light.
Waves of healing soothed my bruised spirit's soul.

Birds of prey fueled a league whose feet
Had dragged in perpetuity; finally finding,
Drinking from the fountain of truth, a people
Dared to pour its waters all over the land.

# At the Table

Scattered upon the presentation,
Broken pauses, shards of glass...
Bold tongues wagging amongst the assemblage.

Yet two came with whisper of a gift...
With joy, they offered a token,
Unraveling paradox of understanding.

Wherever gathered, with silver or gold,
Spotlight shone solely upon the gossipers.
Except for two, each filled with introspection.

Of self-same pride.  Opening wounds, pouring
Salt, the gossipers smugly sang self-same songs.
Presumed their mirrored images superior.

Standing firm, the two, granting reprieves
Presented gifts, issued invitations.  Love,
Forgiving all, tried to make things right.

Some kneeled, some begged pardon for pride
Of attitude  For misdeeds, for slander... the others,
Mute, hungered neither nor thirsted for truth.

# Tzemin
# Ition
# Tsai

Dr. Tzemin Ition Tsai (蔡澤民博士) was born in Republic of China, in 1957. He holds a Ph.D. in Chemical Engineering and two Masters of Science in Applied Mathematics and Chemical Engineering. He is a professor at Asia University (Taiwan), editor of "Reading, Writing and Teaching" academic text. He also writes the long-term columns for Chinese Language Monthly in Taiwan.

He is a scholar with a wide range of expertise, while maintaining a common and positive interest in science, engineering and literature member. He is also an editor of "Reading, Writing and Teaching" academic text and a columnist for *'Chinese Language Monthly'* in Taiwan

He has won many national literary awards. His literary works have been anthologized and published in books, journals, and newspapers in more than 40 countries and have been translated into more than a dozen languages.

# A Smile To River Ducks

I sit here all day
Waiting for the green waves to hit the banks
I listen to the lotus song quietly
Let the melodious rhyme accompany the water breeze
I laughed at the wild ducks
Touching the ship window secretly with a cry
I eavesdrop
Those overlapped green hills has repeatedly advised the surrounding lake
However
I forgot how to open the bow

Lotus flowers are so dense
The waves pushing the sound of flute into the faint fog
Rain tears with twilight tint the spring river
West winds turned into heavy scales all over the surface
How to stop wild ducks from flying over this area again
But the person who planted willows in the past can't be found for a long time
Where he is now?
Can you see it? The wild duck is still there
Can you see it? The wild duck is still there

# That's Just A Path In The Forest

The lion's footsteps are heavy and restless
Sweeping the fallen leaves under one's feet
Inaudible moment
The roar of the lion is like dumb mat grass under the tree
Lying quietly
But know how to cherish the sunlight coming from diagonally

National Referendum Hearing Record
The government should completely ban imports
Pig meat containing beta-receptor hormones ractopamine
The corners of the pursed lips rise
Attempt to show inner disdain
Isn't that one?
Issues that shouldn't be created but inexplicably produced
That's just a path in the forest

National Referendum Hearing Record
The government shouldn't
Attempt to destroy the coast and sea area of Tai Tam algae reef only for the transportation of natural gas
Frowning eyebrows
There is a wolf-like look under the eyes of a pair of eagles
Isn't that one?
Issues that shouldn't be created but inexplicably produced
That's just a path in the forest

The sharp wheel of time
Overwhelming the incisive and terrifying roar of the lion
Force it
To stagger with such a waning pace
The shaky figure melts into the gloomy forest
Dumb cicadas
Go along the only forest path

# Brain Imprint

Waves sway the sea and the moon
Star Shadow Enters the Tower
The night heron is as cold as falling snow at night
Moon bow shadow over the tree
The square fish pond was looked like a mirror without any traces
Like a ruler
Lay out the government's carefully designed policy advocacy
By people's taxes are deeply rooted in government departments

Waves sway the sea and the moon
Star shadow gradually moved into the tower
There are so many disturbances and disputes in our world tonight
Both white-heads and green-sideburns are mad and insane
The world of the Internet, the sharp edge of the government
Domesticated young man
There is no time to talk about the ideals of life
In the past outside the struggle of hatred

This is a fake democratic government
Concealed in the dark and obscure democratic vote counting program
One vote, one vote
Jade storied building, spring's footsteps stop
Looking up at the clouds without moonlight
The hills outside the garden follow the loneliness
The people hope to find the moonlight in chaos
My night herons
Can you not just mind the little fish under your mouth that only has enough to feed your belly?

# Shareef Abdur Rasheed

Shareef Abdur-Rasheed, AKA Zakir Flo was born and raised in Brooklyn, New York. His education includes Brooklyn College, Suffolk County Community College and Makkah, Saudi Arabia. He is a Veteran of the Viet Nam era, where in 1969 he reverted to his now reverently embraced Islamic Faith. He is very active in the Islamic community and beyond with his teachings, activism and his humanity.

Shareef's spiritual expression comes through the persona of "Zakir Flo" . Zakir is Arabic for "To remind". Never silent, Shareef Abdur-Rasheed is always dropping science, love, consciousness and signs of the time in rhyme.

Shareef is the Patriarch of the Abdur-Rasheed Family with 9 Children (6 Sons and 3 Daughters) and 41 Grandchildren (24 Boys and 17 Girls).

For more information about Shareef, visit his personal FaceBook Page at :

https://www.facebook.com/shareef.abdurrasheed1
https://zakirflo.wordpress.com

# Rayen Kang

beauty thing
stamp of approval
isn't on postage
it's your mindset
better yet
your heart
devoted to art
painting water fowl
just a part
your committed to impart
awareness to our obligation
restoration of our water life
maintaining and sustaining
life in all its forms
free of being violated,
disrespected
your commitment to your art
as a vehicle to stimulate
awareness, restore purity
to our waterways, air to breath
the foods we eat and feed
to human beings beginning with
ourselves and those we love
Thank your special young lady.
may you grow and shine in your
art and humanity be a beacon

*food4thought = educucation*

# VERDICT!

came in swift
how else should it
what no acquittal
y'all actually believed your
eyez
is that why folk surprised
a man got to die
cameras rolling
life stolen for nothing
ameriKKKa your f*(k#d up
takes all this time to fess up
when the whole dam world
knew watsup
how else could it be
when humans get taken out
for all to see
watsup ameriKKKa smart phones
smarter than thee?
you still had to try to perpetuate
the lie that Mr. Floyd died because
this 'n ' that trying your a$$ off
lying your a$$ off
to make lies facts but not this time
so, if there was no video, no crime
Chauvin walks, to stork and kill
again
that's what you telling me ameriKKKa?
you heard me! You who came here
to steal, kill, maim in god's name?
way back in the day over 500 years
of days you still the same

steal, lie, kill, maim that other
in god's name?
you despicable, evil, will eventually
be fuel for the flame called HELL
by name
where you will dwell eternally
with the other empire's
in the fire.
oh say can i see?
dam skippy!
and you know thee all seeing
all hearing, all knowing
got something for you
and ooh god
see's all with certainty

*food4thought = educucation*

# Light!

emanates piercing darkness
reflective of truth overpower
falsehood
one little ray of nur(light)
disperses dark ignorance
goes away
can't stay in the company
of bright rays
truth comes and beats the
brains out of falsehood
just as evil is trumped by good
love overpowers hate
such is the power of divine light
rays of truth shine bright
pierce darkness of night
send ignorance to flight
forbid evil enjoins right
assigned to the righteous
this noble plight
this is the purpose of life
created to worship, praise the
creator from where you came
commissioned to glorify his name
hear and obey
remind mankind the words Allah(swt)
say
put that into practice everyday
not the lip service way
words a mirror of your deeds
for you is to be a beacon
lighting the way

a lamp onto the feet
rendering falsehood running away
in full defeat
bearing witness the sound
of Shaitan (Satan) in retreat

*food4thought = education*

# Kimberly Burnham

Kimberly Burnham

A brain health expert with a PhD in Integrative Medicine, Kimberly Burnham has lived in tropical Colombia; in Belgium during the Vietnam War; in Japan teaching businessmen English; in diverse international Toronto, Canada; and several places in the US. Now, she's in Spokane, WA with her wife, Elizabeth, two sets of twins (age 11 & 14) and three dogs. Her recent book, *Awakenings: Peace Dictionary, Language and the Mind, a Daily Brain Health Program* includes the word for peace in hundreds of languages. Her poetry weaves through 80+ volumes of *The Year of the Poet*, *Inspired by Gandhi*, *Women Building the World*, and *A Woman's Place in the Dictionary*. She is currently working on several ekphrastic writing projects. One is a novel, *Art Thief Cracks Healing Code for Parkinson's Disease* and the other is non-fiction, *Using Ekphrastic Fiction Writing and Poetry to Create Interest and Promote Artists, Writers, and Poets*.

http://www.NerveWhisperer.Solutions

https://healthy-brain.medium.com/bears-at-the-window-of-climate-change-d1fb403eeaf3

# Birds Tanka

Don't say birds are more

important people need homes

food love just it'd

be nice when we destroy, plant

a few trees and fruit bushes

# Today

Teal turquoise water

alive with green and blue waves

ducks float endangered

by pollution and a lack

colors a quest to survive

## Saving Them All

Two ducks one real

one potential reflected

as if to say look

care save both realities

with potential in sunlight

Elizabeth
E.
Castillo

## Elizabeth Esguerra Castillo

Elizabeth Esguerra Castillo is a multi-awarded and an Internationally-Published Contemporary Author/Poet and a Professional Writer / Creative Writer / Feature Writer / Journalist / Travel Writer from the Philippines. She has 2 published books, "Seasons of Emotions" (UK) and "Inner Reflections of the Muse", (USA). Elizabeth is also a co-author to more than 60 international anthologies in the USA, Canada, UK, Romania, India. She is a Contributing Editor of Inner Child Magazine, USA and an Advisory Board Member of Reflection Magazine, an international literary magazine. She is a member of the American Authors Association (AAA) and PEN International.

Web links:

Facebook Fan Page

https://free.facebook.com/ElizabethEsguerraCastillo

Google Plus

https://plus.google.com/u/0/+ElizabethCastillo

# The Wonders of Nature

Beloved nature should be conserved,
Blessings from the Source, protect thee
Art captures the beauty of nature
But seeing it for real
Gives us an immense pleasure.
Isn't it a wonder how it all came to be?
When God created the Earth,
Nature was blessed with bounty
Look around you even the waterfowl is a masterpiece
For the Master Artist did it all with love.

# Free the Oppressed

Amid the pandemic, wars loom the land
So where do we go from here,  we ask
When all things seem to fall apart?
Were our prayers being ignored
Why would sufferings continue to prevail
But all these chaos make no sense at all.

Free the oppressed souls pleading for mercy
Reaching out for the sky, crying their hearts out
Spare the innocent ones, the weak and the sick
Free the oppressed begging for love and compassion.

# The Nomad

He had been traveling on foot
Since the time he was a little boy
Getting to nowhere, no direction
The sun was his companion
The moon was his guardian
As he sets his eyes on the Promised Land.
A Nomadic he was, belonging to no one,
The wind carries him anywhere it blows
In the dark night, wolves howl
But he is not one who succumbs to fear.

# Joe
# Paire

# Joe Paire

Joseph L Paire' aka Joe DaVerbal Minddancer . . . is a quiet man, born in a time where civil liberties were a walk on thin ice. He's been a victim of his own shyness often sidelined in his own quest for love. He became the observer, charting life's path. Taking note of the why, people do what they do. His writings oft times strike a cord with the dormant strings of the reader. His pen the rosined bow drawn across the mind. He comes full-frontal or in the subtlest way, always expressing in a way that stimulate the senses.

www.facebook.com/joe.minddancer

# Waterfowl

I'm in this scene of cool water and ripples.
My distorted reflection allows me to check my feathers.
Funny isn't it, funny it's not.
There are others to listen to.

This sky beneath me this guy beneath me.
Are swallows followed like me?
I see the blind men hidden deep within the trees.
No lead for me today, what's left for me to say?

Wait, is that a fly, with a Day-Glo line attached to it.
Faith is blind but few believe and just scratch through it.
Flannel shirts and waders, Florida alligators.
I find solitude in the calm of the day.

The eddy's tickle a bit as I spot a tiny fin.
a few of my buddies are flying in.
It's feeding time and the water is teaming.
Fluorescent features on my feathers.

I think I'm being written in a poem.
I think I'd rather not be stuffed.
I've never been a fan of pillows.
And please don't say Foie gras.

# Outside Now

Restrictions are lifted
still I sit here in my home.
I'm not one for outside
the outside has no room.
I need at least.
six miles of separation
Slick smiles adapt at taking.
My personal prison.

I'm living my liven.
Society has these funny rules.
You have to interact
to be considered cool.
Status quo foolishness
how can you make rules to this
survival of the Bible
people rarely use the truth in it.

Step by step in chronological order
educate graduate, marry someone's daughter.
have a few kids, and complain about disorder.
After all that, can I have my borders.
I'm not going to a senior's function
to prove I still function.
back when the masks had everyone upset
I was the happiest I've ever been.

Feathering relations where I never should have been.
Three hots and a cot are all I need.
Internet connection and a wide screen TV.
Who am I kidding, I just don't fit?

# My Sunsets Are Beautiful

It’s a spring thing for a time.
I try to catch the glow of me.
Church steeples block private communication.
Conversations with my God and I
My god, I have captured what can’t be seen.
Every day it seems there’s a pattern.
The birds pose for me now.
I’m learning their language.
I spoke in Blue Jay and he landed in my frame.
I got a shot of wings tail and everything.
five o’clock shadows wait until nine.
I can’t get a clear shot past these powerlines.
The blue jay chased a crow.
no matter how many breadcrumbs I throw.
I can only catch the sunset from front row.

# hülya n. yılmaz

Information

Professor Emerita (Humanities, Penn State, USA), hülya n. yılmaz [sic] is a published tri-lingual author, literary translator, and Director of Editing Services (Inner Child Press International, USA). Her work has appeared in numerous anthologies of global endeavors and was presented at poetry events in the U.S. and abroad. In 2018, the WIN of British Colombia, Canada honored yılmaz with a literary excellence award. Her two poems remain permanently installed in *Telepoem Booth* (USA). hülya finds it vital for everyone to understand a deeper sense of self, and writes creatively to attain a comprehensive awareness for and development of our humanity.

Writing Web Site
https://hulyanyilmaz.com/

Editing Web Site
https://hulyasfreelancing.com

# snail mail

tucked in inside various kinds of envelopes,
postcards and personal (or professional) letters
donned their two-option stamp:
domestic or international

they are now on their way
to become a mere memory
of the fast-disappearing past

long before emails won the popularity contest
having gained a steady support
at a record-breaking speed,
snail mail used to be the long-distance venue
with its two-option destination:
domestic or international

if you are my age,
you too have probably seen many a stamp
some, uplifting in their flower prints
or season-specific images;
others, destined to mark awareness
for many a fatal disease

who recalls ever seeing the Duck Stamp
of the U.S. Postal Services in 2020?
i do not, nor did i know about its significance
as far as helping people conserve wildlife
or its contribution to the visibility
of educational programs in the United States,
those that focused solely on largely neglected issues
of environmental and conservation concerns

yet . . . for years – clueless
about the notable mark of the Duck Stamp,
i have been donating to the one leading U.S. organization –
well-known in its efforts in this arena

clueless no more . . .

# my beloved grandfather

he was still young enough to climb up and down
those multiple steep concrete steps

the most exciting part of his every single day
would announce itself with the arrival of the mailman

after his historically unique private home,
he lived in an upper-most flat of an apartment complex

the mailboxes were right at the entry of the building
down, way down the seemingly unending stairway

he would rush to get to that floor,
hoping that his children or grandchildren
had written to him once more

when i visited him the last time,
he mistook me for my Mom
and my daughter, for me

Alzheimer's had become his steady companion,
along with the postcards he long ago secured
with his longing and love on his self-made pin board

# lonely mailboxes

promotions galore

junk mail, occupying space

emptiness inside

# Teresa
# E.
# Gallion

Teresa E. Gallion was born in Shreveport, Louisiana and moved to Illinois at the age of 15. She completed her undergraduate training at the University of Illinois Chicago and received her master's degree in Psychology from Bowling Green State University in Ohio. She retired from New Mexico state government in 2012.

She moved to New Mexico in 1987. While writing sporadically for many years, in 1998 she started reading her work in the local Albuquerque poetry community. She has been a featured reader at local coffee houses, bookstores, art galleries, museums, libraries, Outpost Performance Space, the Route 66 Festival in 2001 and the State of Oklahoma's Poetry Festival in Cheyenne, Oklahoma in 2004. She occasionally hosts an open mic.

Teresa's work is published in numerous Journals and anthologies. She has two CDs: *On the Wings of the Wind* and *Poems from Chasing Light*. She has published three books: *Walking Sacred Ground, Contemplation in the High Desert* and *Chasing Light.*

*Chasing Light* was a finalist in the 2013 New Mexico/Arizona Book Awards.

The surreal high desert landscape and her personal spiritual journey influence the writing of this Albuquerque poet. When she is not writing, she is committed to hiking the enchanted landscapes of New Mexico. You may preview her work at

***http://bit.ly/1aIVPNq*** or ***http://bit.ly/13IMLGh***

# The Emperor Has Feathers

White fuzz covers his head,
rolls down the back of his neck,
flows into a sea of blue variants
that signify his status as emperor goose.

His image reflected in the water
sends out waves of color to attract girls.
Nature has its own way of doing things
in the natural world.

No girl in the pond would give him
a first nor second glance
if he had no colorful features
to showcase his beauty.

# Soul Serenade

The sermons come daily
bubbling and gurgling
over stones that listen
until perfectly smooth waterfalls
dance in small portions.

The theme of the sermons
is peace and harmony,
steadfast commitment,
power and strength
to move forward
no matter what happens.

Many come to the river
but do not hear the sound current
nor see the spiritual light.
They are spiritually unconscious.

The breeze is always a song.
If we learn to listen,
the Soul will be serenaded
into an awakening.

# Joshua Tree Therapist

My therapist spoke to me through
a culture of trees called Joshua.
I spoke back bending my knees
in humility and the trees anointed me
with love in a praise song
filled with laughter and mischief.

One said to me,
how do you like my sexy afro?
My nappy needles draw attention
when I bend in my fashion pose.

Come close.
You have earned the privilege
to hug me with grace and gratitude.

How could I resist an ecstatic touch?
I hugged it and said,
I love you.

Ashok
K.
Bhargava

Ashok Bhargava is a poet, writer, community activist, public speaker, management consultant and a keen photographer. Based in Vancouver, he has published several collections of his poems: Riding the Tide, Mirror of Dreams, A Kernel of Truth, Skipping Stones, Half Open Door and Lost in the Morning Calm. His poetry has been published in various literary magazines and anthologies.

Ashok is a Poet Laureate and poet ambassador to Japan, Korea and India. He is founder of WIN: Writers International Network Canada. Its main objective is to inspire, encourage, promote and recognize writers of diverse genres, artists and community leaders. He has received many accolades including Nehru Humanitarian Award for his leadership of Writers International Network Canada, Poets without Borders Peace Award for his journeys across the globe to celebrate peace and to create alliances with poets, and Kalidasa Award for creative writings.

## World of Senses

lush surroundings
soft silky touch
a carefree goose
glides on dark green waters

the midday sun on my skin
the wild wood fragrance
wafts
embraces mother earth

dragonflies dart
a hummingbirds
hover
soft shadows

the infinite perfection
conveyed to physical senses
to fishes in the deep
birds in the sky

the morning dew on grass
beneath my bare feet
at every moment of every day
even now

if it weren't for you
such ecstasies
I would never
Know

# Morning Walk

Red poppies
A sense of solitude
In the air

Behind the trees
The sun rises
Trickle down
Rays of hope
Like a silk sari flutter

I recall her name
In a void of nothingness
As butterflies and birds
Hurry
To their routine

## Keepers of Faith

I observe
How a seed
Sprouts
Seasons
And births
Seeds

No regrets
No complaints
Only green smiles

I imitate
Grow
Bloom
And then …

This is
How to live

Graciously with
Sky
Forest
River and
Land

I am delighted to see
such
a breath of fresh air

# Caroline 'Ceri Naz' Nazareno Gabis

# Carolin 'Ceri' Nazareno-Gabis

Caroline 'Ceri Naz' Nazareno-Gabis, author of Velvet Passions of Calibrated Quarks, World Poetry Canada International Director to Philippines is known as a 'poet of peace and friendship', a multi-awarded poet, editor, journalist, speaker, linguist, educator, peace and women's advocate. She believes that learning other's language and culture is a doorway to wisdom.

Among her poetic belts include PANORAMA YOUTH LITERARY AWARDS 2020, 7 th Prize Winner in the 19th, 20th and 21st Italian Award of Literary Festival; Writers International Network-Canada "Amazing Poet 2015", The Frang Bardhi Literary Prize 2014 (Albania), the sair-gazeteci or Poet Journalist Award 2014 (Tuzla, Istanbul, Turkey) and World Poetry Empowered Poet 2013 (Vancouver, Canada). She's a featured member of Association of Women's Rights and Development (AWID), The Poetry Posse, Galaktika Poetike, Asia Pacific Writers and Translators (APWT ), Axlepino and Anacbanua.

Her poetry and children's stories have been featured in different anthologies and magazines worldwide.

Links to her works:

panitikan.ph/2018/03/30/caroline-nazareno-gabis

apwriters.org/author/ceri_naz/

www.aveviajera.org/nacionesunidasdelasletras/id1181 .html

# Promises at the Duck Pond River

I was at the end of the bridge
While you gently come and surprise me
With the pan de sal and hot rice coffee
We ambushed the silence of the pond,
You and I throwing stones
Like innocents, and count while ducks play
In search of their mother to swim over the hills.
There was a sudden silence,
You embraced me like there's no tomorrow and space.
I was like the statue of liberty
Unmoved.
I just can feel the sincerest hugs and promises
You have whispered,
''You complete me'',
Soothing days are simple days
Holding you at the river pond's end.

# Dulcinea

Impressed ''to go beyond
the ordinary''
seeing possibilities,
looking greatness,
committing to  believe
that dreams come true,
that goals in life reflects purity
and undying.

Inspired to live beyond
To heal the land,
While requiem is sang
From the mountains of the free
Distance between my wings
To the rainbow's gold
Has flown to reach
A million words!

# Hammock of Love

It sways while singing melancholic hums
Tied from two strong poles
Like your arms tied around my neck
And gently hold your back to
Calm the tides from your heart,
As it sways back and forth,
I think of the memories left
and remained untouched.
Intangible clips of real movies
Like our first fairy tale,
That was shadowless preview
From the chains of the hammock,
It keeps the rope firm
Like my faith to you,
It sways  to brilliant joys
Like how I deeply feel
For your tender love.

# Swapna Behera

## Swapna Behera

Swapna Behera is a bilingual contemporary poet, author, translator and editor from Odisha, India. She was a teacher from 1984 to 2015. Her stories, poems and articles are widely published in National and International journals, and ezines, and are translated into different national and International languages. She has penned six books. She is the recipient of the Prestigious International Mother Language UGADI AWARD WINNER 2019. She was conferred upon the Prestigious International Poesis Award of Honor at the 2nd Bharat Award for Literature as Jury in 2015, The Enchanting Muse Award in India World Poetree Festival 2017, World Icon of Peace Award in 2017, and the Pentasi B World Fellow Poet in 2017. She is the recipient of the Prolific Poetess Award ,The Life time Achievement Award ,The Best Planner Award ,The Sahitya Shiromani Award, ATAL BIHARI BAJPAYEE Award, ATAL Award 2018 ,Global Literature Guardian Award ,International Life Time Achievement Award and the Master of Creative Impulse Award .She has received the Honoured Poet of India from the Seychelles Government accredited Literary Society Lasher one poem A NIGHT IN THE REFUGEE CAMP is translated into 60 languages .She is the Ambassador of Humanity by Hafrikan Prince Art World Africa 2018 and an official member of World Nation's Writers Union ,Kazakhstan2018. Italy, the National President for India by Hispanomundial Union of Writers (UHE), Peru, the administrator of several poetic groups, and the Cultural Ambassador for India and South Asia of Inner Child Press African is the life member of Odisha Environmental Society.

swapna.behera@gmail.com

# and she is the winner

a small duck

with slender bill

the crest and hood

that dives in fresh water ponds

an  acrylic painting

of an emperor goose

the art of Rayen King

the young stamp artist

won the Georgia Junior Duck stamp contest

# i am still standing in a line

i am still standing in a line
i am standing still in the line
no one moves not even the pedestrians, cyclists
florists, neither a teacher nor a student
my city is stand and still
except the virulent virus
the street dogs are hungry,
there is panic and terror
media transmitting fear, cries
seminars, graveyards, doctors, vaccines
foreign help for oxygen
military is active
i am standing
against the silent minions
building my sky
reconstructing the unlocked world
the dead calendar flings on the wall of a parliament
golden memories are in the iron chest
or in the casket
when time twists
eyes deposit empty dreams
the artist sells vegetables
the painter sells masks
hugging, jogging and celebration all over
here a pyre, there a pyre
every where a long line
on line and off line for oxygen
hospital beds are full
people talk about ventilator, virus
capsules and I.C.U.s
it seems there is terrible disorder

i am waiting for that day
when music bands will march forward
on the national highway
to detoxify the air
migrants will get a plate full of rice
every living being will be without masks
yes, hunger opens the masks
and covers the face too
my pen and prayer all I have
they are walking from this time zone to the other
to be ordained and work for next generation
I am waiting and waiting ......
inside a machine

# the lady Tarzan

the lady Tarzan
guards the lush green forests
from mafias and naxalites
protects forests
creates awareness
she is fearless
bold and determined
she and her gang of women
with arrows, sickles, sticks
shout and fight
raise the voice for the trees
"don't ever dare to touch the leaves
our jungle; our life"
ten thousand women
sow the saplings to create forests
the community protects
she the fearless, firebrand leader
bride of Jharkhand
village after village she walked
formed the groups
to guard the forest day and night
trees are friends
so, they tied holy strings to protect
she is fearless
an environmental activist
for forest conservation
a truly empowered woman
standing boldly
among the trees
Jamuna Tudu, the lady Tarzan ......

Jharkhand;- Jharkhand is a state of India

# Albert 'Infinite' Carrasco

Albert "Infinite The Poet" Carrasco is an urban poet, mentor and public speaker.

Albert believes his experience of growing up in poverty, dealing with drugs and witnessing murder over and over were lessons learnt, in order to gain knowledge to teach. Albert's harsh reality and honesty is a powerfully packed punch delivered through rhyme. Infinite grew up in the east part of the Bronx and still resides there, so he knows many young men will follow the same dark path he followed looking for change. The life of crime should never be an option to being poor but it is, very often.

Infinite poetry @lulu.com

Alcarrasco2 on YouTube

Infinite the poet on reverbnation

## Infinite Poetry

http://www.lulu.com/us/en/shop/al-infinite-carrasco/infinite-poetry/paperback/product-21040240.html

# Rayen Kang (duck on a stamp)

i see freedom on wisdom.

i can fly away but floating,

riding this current is where i'll stay.

The wisdom couldn't be any clearer,

its as if its my own rippled mirror.

My surroundings are beautiful and it is accented by this peaceful river.

Air is above me and theres an array of fish beneath my belly,

I am in the middle of beauty.

sun beams as i go downstream,

I'm warm on top and underneath I'm cool like the swimming... schools.

At the moment my destination isn't clear

so right now i'll soak in this jaw dropping scenery

until I'm placed on the top right of an envelope being sent to an addressee

# We are not the same

I'm an eighties crack baby, we're not the same. Dudes are hustl'n, I am the game. Inf watched the forefathers mix the cement for the foundation, my reign was meant, I wasn't lucky, standing on the top was intended, them brick layers knew I'll grow to be what was built future superintendent. In the school of hard knocks I was an exchange student, I saw them come, I saw the hand to hand, I saw them leave, before I even touched work I was sale fluent.

I saw the beef and witnessed the wars for breaking code of the street laws, saw stacks on top of stacks when I was still poor. I had next, there was no bleachers to sit on, in order to learn the ropes I had to stand side by side men pushn Coke and her-ron. I became a product of my environment since I was surrounded by mobsters, when my turn came up I was a monster.

Shit was fly'n, slugs and oil that turned to rock while still in hot water, wasn't a wait-er, i was a hungry go getter so I stood in that lobby takn orders. no one was taking what was built from me, I'm holding shit down, I prayed that I didn't have to be the reason why someone is holding down balance beams in physical therapy.

There was a lot to prove and a lot to lose so ya had to make an example of the first violator so the rest respect how ya move. I'm getting locked up but coming right back, I getting raided back to back, got hit up and came right back, poverty was behind me and no matter what, I wasn't looking back. All my failure made me better, trials and tribulations were just education on becoming a high-school valedictorian that will earn his masters.

Regardless to all my brilliance and intelligence I couldn't solve the algorithm that'll end the slug violence that left many men close to me infinitely silenced. I've grown with soldiers that lived by the gun and died by killers shootn one, I had to live hypocritical because I didn't want to have to repeat my hardest fight of fighting to emerge from critical to stable. We are not the same, I watched the forefathers mix the cement that built the foundation for a place I lived... The house of pain.

## Near death

I've been through so many near death experiences that I used to tell myself, al you one lucky man! and I knew I had a purpose, this writing game had yet to surface. I survived attempts of assassination, hurdled over trials and tribulation, got wheeled in hospitals on gurneys, a few days later i walked out of emergency. got arrested and bailed out before incarceration, I road my chariot filled with lives through the fire and emerged on the other side as a solo rider, i said bye to many men before burial or cremation. I learnt my purpose. the words I write provoke emotion when spoken, Ive been chosen to speak about drugs, jail and murder, because most of my life was about drugs jail and murder. They say it takes a village to raise a child, well I'm a project life villager trying to intercept children from living vile, before reaching rikers isle, or laying like I was in montefiore in critical.

# Eliza Segiet

Eliza Segiet: Master's Degree in Philosophy, completed postgraduate studies in Cultural Knowledge, Philosophy, Arts and Literature at Jagiellonian University. She is a member of The Association of Polish Writers and The NWNU - Union of Writers of the World.

Her poems *Questions* and *Sea of Mists* won the title of the International Publication of the Year 2017 and 2018 in Spillwords Press.

For her volume of *Magnetic People* she won a literary award of a *Golden Rose* named after Jaroslaw Zielinski (Poland 2019 r.). Her poem The *Sea of Mists* was chosen as one of the best one hundred poems of 2018 by International Poetry Press Publication Canada.
In Poet's Yearbook, as the author of *Sea of Mists*, she was awarded with the prestigious Elite Writer's Status Award as one of the best poets of 2019 (July 2019).
She was awarded *World Poetic Star Award* by World Nations Writers Union – the world's largest Writers' Union from Kazakhstan (August 2019).
In September 2019 she was 1st Place Laureate (Foreign Poetry category) – in Contest *Quando È la Vita ad Invitare* for poem *Be Yourself* (Italy).
Her poem *Order* from volume *Unpaired* was selected as one of the 100 best poems of 2019 in International Poetry Press Publications (Canada).
Nominated for the Pushcart Prize 2019.
Nominated for the iWoman Global Awards (2019).
Laureate Naji Naaman Literary Prize 2020.
Laureate International Award PARAGON OF HOPE (Canada, 2020).
Obtained certificate of appreciation from *Gujarat Sahitya Academy* and *Motivational Strips* for literary excellence par with global standards (2020).
Ambassador of Literature granted by *Motivational Strips*.
Author's works can be found in anthologies, separate books and literary magazines worldwide.

# Dead vestige

*To Rayen Kang*

Stop, human!
Don't destroy our home,
don't take the territory.
Do you think
we want to live in puffs of smog?
We need the nature,
not words
about environmental protection.

You can take photos of us,
turn them into stamps, pics, decorations
- it's but a mere copy of ourselves.
We can fly, run, swim...
We don't want to be only
a dead vestige,
an ornament in our destroyers' sham paradise.

To amuse for centuries
we have to live.

*Translated by Ula de B.*

# Kingdom

Man-doomed
trees
have no voice.

They are silent.

They stop being
the Green Lungs of the World.

They become just wood
that does not help Earth,
an extinguished
kingdom of breath

– a void of destroyers!

*Translated by Artur Komoter*

# Trampoline

Doesn't plan,
but inanely strives towards the goal
– the death of the Earth.
Forgets that lands, seas, oceans
are places of life.
The trampoline to their annihilation is
the human
– once called *homo sapiens,*
today....

Better to remain silent.

*Translated by Piotr Karczewski*

# William S. Peters Sr.

Bill's writing career spans a period of over 50 years. Being first Published in 1972, Bill has since went on to Author in excess of 50 additional Volumes of Poetry, Short Stories, etc., expressing his thoughts on matters of the Heart, Spirit, Consciousness and Humanity. His primary focus is that of Love, Peace and Understanding!

Bill says . . .

I have always likened Life to that of a Garden. So, for me, Life is simply about the Seeds we Sow and Nourish. All things we "Think and Do", will "Be" Cause and eventually manifest itself to being an "Effect" within our own personal "Existences" and "Experiences" . . . whether it be Fruit, Flowers, Weeds or Barren Landscapes! Bill highly regards the Fruits of his Labor and wishes that everyone would thus go on to plant "Lovely" Seeds on "Good Ground" in their own Gardens of Life!

to connect with Bill, he is all things Inner Child

www.iaminnerchild.com

Personal Web Site

www.iamjustbill.com

# So much more

From Nature

To inspiration

To concept

To color

To canvas

To museums

To Collections

To vaults

To magazines, to books to newspapers

To classrooms

To Cities, to countries

I have travelled

And now I am a beautiful stamp

And still

So much more

# Listen . . . Observe

I heard things in the silence
Whispers in the fray
I saw movement in the stillness
And darkness in each day

You are never empty my dear,
Even if it appears so

There is a joy hidden
In all sorrows
Hope can be found
For all tomorrows
The beggar begs
We all borrow
From life and its abundance

Let us dance
With abandon
And an unabashed mirth,
Simply being jovial
Because we can

I sing praises unto
My unknown self
Which we term
As God
Or something other

In the stillness
There is movement
And I embrace
That which it teaches

Everywhere I look,
There is a poem
Waiting for me,
For you,
To pay attention,
And perhaps transcribe
Into a consciousness
You understand,
And may possibly share
With others

Seek they say,
And you shall find,
But first,
Let us define
Exactly what we are seeking . . .
…..
Is it peace?
Is it love?
Is it abundance?
What may it be,
That sates one's soul?

Does Death hold the answers
We fear to face?
Does love of another
Fix the loneliness we feel within?
…..
What, tell me
What is it we celebrate
At the birth of a child . . .
Every newborne? . . .

Are all lights
Destined to go out ?
Do all journeys have
A destination?
Do all songs end?
How long does the music play?

Listen . . . Observe

# Soft things

A whisper, a languid breath,
A lingering caress,
A soft smile
Full of wrinkles
Around the eyes
Delicate fragrances and
Gentle aromatic scents,
A child's look of wonder,
The rhythmic music of your heart.

These are the things
That come to mind
And infiltrate my spirit
That chase all traces
Of angst away

Soft things

# June
# 2021
# Featured Poets

~ * ~

Alonzo "zO" Gross

Lali Tsipi Michaeli

Tareq al Karmy

Tirthendu Ganguly

I
Fly
because
I Can
. . . said the Dreamer to the world.
www.iamjustbill.com

# Alonzo
# "zO"
# Gross

# Alonzo 'zO' Gross

Alonzo "zO" Gross or zO-AlonzO is a songwriter, Dancer, recording artist and writer.

His short stories were first published internationally in 2005 and in 2006 in the Staying Sane book series published by Evelyn Fazio. Staying Sane when family comes to visit (2005) and Staying Sane during the Thanksgiving Holiday. His first book of poems entitled **Inspiration, Harmony and the World Within** was published in 2012. Also in that same year he was awarded "Best Spoken Word Poet" at the Lehigh Valley music awards. In 2016 zO was selected as a featured poet in the film "VOICES" directed by Gina Nemo filmed in Los Angeles California and released in 2017 in select theatres as well as Amazon Prime. Then in January of 2018 he released his second book of poetry entitled "**sOuL eLiXir The writingZ of zO"** which was greeted with rave reviews and a 5 out of 5 star rating. In November 2020 zO was named as one of the best poets of 2020 by Inner Child Press where his work was featured in their Anthology. In June of 2021 zO released his highly antcipated 3rd book of poetry/art entitled "**PoemZ 4 U AND YourZ"** available globally. zO is a graduate in the field of English Literature from Temple University, and looks forward to releasing music cds as well as new books of poetry and art.

# Breaking "The Amnesia"...

Was it a past vision?
Or from this plane,
did i briefly pass/?
As i beheld,
unknown colors of a prism
Betwixt the strange
bewitching grass/.
Coiled Neatly,
Neath my feet light as mist °
Soiled Sweetly,
the cherub blades blowin'
Ever so gently
and yet gracefully brisk °.
Twas then,
The Angel Michael,
(Speaking dreamily sublime)
From the portal ^
or was it Heaven ?
(as if reading my mind)
said unto me
(in a manner so cordial) ^
Dearest Goddess
as U R in this Expression
Tell me
what is time,
in this paradigm
Of Infinitely Infinite Immortals?" ^
(But before i could fathom the question).
My ears,
heard the Wondrous soundZ °
Of Inumeral ViolinZ
singin' Ever Verily Profound °
4 whilst once wounded,
and cocooned

in my internal war,
i found °
"oneness" in 7 billions starZ
performing rapturous melodies
A most ecstasy filled score
Twere as if,
each note bore a Crown. °👑
I applauded, cheered
with mine soul,
in Delightful Ovation `
Under a shade,
of the bluest parasol,
I saw,
in the clear
Mine ancestors of Ev'ry generation `
(ancient and young)
speaking
(without tongue)
engaged in quiet telepathic conversation. ´
Then i would i hear a voice
Coming from some near
distant-distinct vicinity <>
"In a blink thou shalt awaken
From this timeless sea of infinity. <>
4 In thy most tulmultous moments
Tis i,
thy net for thy ev'ry fall {}
As mine Love has covered thee
even whilst in thy infancy ye crawled {}
Now Arise,
In New Birth
& in verse
Doeth recall {}
with thy newness of heart and eyeZ,
All thou hath felt and saw". {}

# God or Schizophrenia... [The Conversation]

Sittin' on the stairZ/
Dark NightZ in my Prayers/
Speakin aloud 2 God,
askin' "why o' why
are thingZ so dang hard!!!?".
"It won't kill u" (A Voice Said)
"I am merely showing u the real u".
Wait. What? was this all in my head?
"Yes & No,
I give u shortcomings,
2 help thee 2 GROW".
"God?" "Yup, whatever u wanna call me
ur Miracle of Life, ur sight, ur light (thas right)
It's all me ". "Expressing me through u,
I give mine Blessings 4 u 2 do what u do.
"Ok God but i don't know how much more i can take,
& how are u so sure that i'm not goin' 2 break?".
"Because i see All, Past, Present
as well as thingZ 2 come,
Wherefore i know though u fall,
u shalt rise as the Sun". "Lord can i be frank?
("I already know that u Will")
"Why are so many good people gettin killed?"
"Everyone has a date, thas all i can say,
plus ur Human Mind couldn't fathom plans Divine anyway"
just know i will give u long long life, Prosperity, Health,
Children & A Beautiful Wife"
"Many of these things have already come ta pass,
share ur Gifts with the World,
that is all that i ask"

"4 i Blessed u with them,
so that u could be a Blessing, my words
through u, Will help others whom art
stressing". "Everything that happened
(my son) is meant 2 be, just know the Lord (ur God)
"Shalt haveth no coward EVER represent me".
Tears in my eyes, i arose from the stairZ/
redeemed it seemed,
Dark NightZ in my Prayers/.
No more
Panic and Cold Stares/
Manic or Mania°
Church or Asylum
God or Schizophrenia°.

# Cutz...(Part 1)

One Cut 4 the anger,
the betrayal
my rage*
4 Cutz 4 the stranger,
who molested me,
4 years of age*.
2 Cutz 4 my daddy,
who I Loved but was killed-
3 Cutz i do (madly)
for many dreamZ unfulfilled-.
2 Cutz 4 my ex °
who only wanted me 4 sex °
who beat me down,
then knocked me up,
only ta never return my texts °.
U see,
I hide my scars,
behind long shirtz & sweaterZ ~
I've blacked out,
seen starZ,
I've bled & hurt,
amidst the stormyest of weather ~.
Anyway,
2 Cutz 4 the family,
that jeers & doubtz me <>
1 cut 4 my grammy,
whom was Sincere,
& the only one,
who cared about me <>.
3 cutz on my leg,
(now those kinda hurt')

1 cut 4 havin' 2 beg,
my abusive pimp 4 work'.
I know i need help,
And somewhere,
True Love is Beaming -------
but still,
i cut maself deep ...
jus tryina find,
the deeper meaning -------.

# Lali
# Tsipi
# Michaeli

# Lali Tsipi Michaeli

**Lali Tsipi Michaeli** is an Israeli independent universal poet. Born in Georgia in 1964. She immigrated to Israel at the age of seven. She has published six poetry books so far. Attended international poetry festivals. She was part of a residecy program for talented writers in New York at 2018.

Her books have been translated into foreign languages in New York,

India, France, Italy, Georgia, Ukraina, Russa, Romania and Iran. Lali was defined by Prof. Gabriel Moked in his book as "Erotico-Urban Poet" and was highly regarded by critics, who consider her as an innovative and combative. In 2011 Lali conducted an anthology for protest "Resistance", in which she presents her personal poetic manifesto, claiming that "poetry as a whole is a revolt." In the past decade, Lali has created 15 Poetry Video Art that have taken part in world poetry festivals such as ZEBRA in Berlin. "The poem is not purely individual. It is common ground and should be heard in a great voice," the poet claims.

Lali teaches Hebrew at Ben Gurion University. She has one son and lives in Tel Aviv by the sea.

## My secret lover, you

An anarchist who corrects me
His language into my language
The one who will not see me on his land
The one that I will not see on my land
But our voices are floating
Like bombardments in the world
Your history is written
In ink that was produced
In the factory of my love.

*tr. from Hebrew Michael Simkin*

## A Poem For A Palestinian Poet

Dear Tareq,

I serve you my poem like a piece of bloody flesh from the brink of my torn body.
Midnight between us marks a line.
You argue "I am from here" and ask me
Where are you from? Where are you from?
Don't you live on my land?
Wind carries away my years of noise in this beast of a country. It leads my feet to walk in this world, washing me from the breast of mother earth.
Me? Do you want to know where I'm from?
I'm from here.
Yes, I have been here for generations. From the dusty royal history, I'm from here.
Meanwhile my brothers are executed everywhere around the globe. Do you know their history?
Do you know what was here before you stepped on this earth?
Before your grandfather plowed this land?
You say that your lands were stolen.
That's right, they were. And on a human level, I am sorry.
I hurt and I understand your wound. But forgive me because I am haunted and I'm asking to return to my safe land.
I am a Jew. This is my only country.
As I wandered far away I was persecuted by another nation, another religion.
I walked with my certainty severed, my land decapitated.
This might be your motherland, but mine have been the water, the dust, the rock and sandstone for 5000 years.
Here I was marked. Here my fate was decided for generations. I was banished from here. Prayed for this place. Longed.

I hid my identity in exile in order to save myself. To
reconnect with the mob of the people that remained for me.
This is where my visa was issued to, where the Soviet
Union said to me for years "Niet".
And anyway, I share with you your sorrow. It is mine too.
How did you sleep? You ask me in a WhatsApp message
right before morning. Before the sun yawned.
My dream has traveled the world. It crossed oceans, wadis
and vineyards. Jumped over walls, contracts and shreds of
war. Unforgiveness speaks in many foreign languages.
Only love had one language.
I too am chased by shadows. I too am a victim wearing the
mask of the victor.
Write, poet! Write everything!
I spill my tears into your ink and with your tears I
punctuate my writing.
Poetry is the only autonomy left in a darkening world.
The only bit of freedom. The only place. The only
redeeming. Though you don't acknowledge salvation.
You are an anarchist after all, believing in the scarred hand
and mostly in love.
Willing to meet me even if historically I am your enemy.
How do you sleep, my friend?
Did you eat?
What are you doing now?
And what are you?
I'm playing the piano, look.
I'm playing the flute, listen.
We'll talk.
We'll talk.

*tr. from Hebrew Maayan Eitan*

# Sulh صلحة

For all those infected months
we witnessed the withering of souls
when the precious body wraps its two banks
as if we were a *Christo* and *Jeanne-Claude* project
in the Middle East.
But she's dead and he's dead
and only a target is left of them
and of us
the suspicion turned into desire that turned into compassion
that turned into alienation
and blocking on social media
as if we were back again at the communication terms
of the year in which this earth was
renamed. The development of a new language out of life
itself
*Ana bahebbak ya qalbi hayati*
I learned the enemy's tongue so I could read the love
poems you wrote me
in moments of envisioning the apocalypse
not normalization but
*sulh*
not the usual matter of things but
a condition of separating from the ground
we both know,
that when fire whispers
the one who made you fall
is the only one who would help you rise up.

***Sulh** صلحة - in Arabic means Resolution*

*tr. from Hebrew by Maayan Eitan*

# Tareq al Karmy

Tareq al Karmy

**Tareq al Karmy**, 1975, a Palestinian poet from the city of Tulkarm. He published 11 poetry files so far. Plays a Nay flute. His poems have been translated into various languages and he has participated in local and international poetry festivals. Al Karmy's poems attempt to write poems without ending, in a way that creates a deliberate interruption in the poem, leaving space for the reader to engage in writing the ending of the poem and leaving him space for imagination. This is a unique and unusual act in the landscape of Palestinian poetry that makes al Karmy one of the most interesting young voices in contemporary Palestinian poetry.

## On a rainy night

You come tired even of me

Let me sleep under your skin and meow

Close your eyes, turn off the house

To finally fall asleep

close your eyes

So I am ...

The rain is burning and

the window is pouring

...

*At night / winter Tulkarm

# My heart is a bell of your secret love

Here you are, under my skin, a sleeping tremor
You milked the dawn in your perfume bottle
Behold, I love you my heart
My fingers blindly penetrate through a fence
To pick you up
Your fingers dip it in the new Berlin Wall
To pick me the coal flower
Did I change the flute between my glowing fingers?
Your fingers are all beaks
Under these fingers I'm
Never tired piano
And from the clash of our fingers we are born...
You are a bell and I am a bell
We knock on each other in all silence...

*Evening / Tulkarem

## The Legend of Mythic, Proud Perfection

Not Richard's – not your "Lionheart" 's – horse, no
Nor Great Alexander's steed Bucephalus, no
Not Roman horses thundering home their demonic mastery,
Not the legendary, immortal, Trojan horse,
No, there's never been a horse on all the earth but –
failing to attain absolute perfection of nobility –
has, in the end, had to be put down
by merciful bullets. Not one
except
this, the one my father bought me,
my horse,
although it's only wee and made of wood.

# Tirthendu Ganguly

Tirthendu Ganguly

**Tirtha** (a.k.a. Tirthendu Ganguly) is the author of the internationally best-selling poetry book, '***Firefly of Love***' (ISBN: 9781794652149). It is published in 13 countries (including USA and UK). His poetry and fictions have been published in various internationally reputed anthologies and journals. In 2016, he received **Vidyasagar Memorial Award** for academic excellence. At present, he is a **Ph.D. Research Scholar** in **English Literature** at **Banaras Hindu University (BHU)** in India. He was also sponsored by **Oxford Centre for Hindu Studies (Oxford University)** to explore the Vedas and Upanishads.

# Let the Lotus Bloom

From *mūlādhāra* to Mount Kailāsa's icy cliff
Let my verse echo this song:
Rhine's azure stream shall flow, hold belief,
Even if all in life is wrong.

The *loo* air of Thar let thy *svādhiṣṭhāna* hold,
And *maṇipūra* be green!
We may sleep unfed, but like a Bengal tiger bold
Soundless, silent, serene!

You may be hurt, but thy *anāhata* must never be so,
Like the Lancashire lovers!
On and on the flow of breath, like Volga, must go
Before it *viśuddha* covers.

From there, slowly roam like the Japanese deer
To the *ājñā* that commands,
Where the purest vibe of creation becomes sheer
Which from *sahasrāra* lands.

Let this be the only path of the human conscience
If we are to erase our gloom:
To find peace in a world that always twists and spins
Let the lotus bloom.

# How many?

How many flowers do bloom in your garden?
Do they all forever stay?
How many words have meanings that we pen
Before the feelings fade away?

How many wintry blows must we all endure
To pave the path for spring?
How many thoughts must a syllable allure
To match the carol that you sing?

How many oceans can a broken ship sail
Unless its wounds are mended?
How many heart-breaks must one life entail
Before it is truly ended?

How many flights must a lonely bird fly
As an ethereal marshal?
How many deaths, how many, must a poet die
To make his love immortal?

## To the Dark Lord

I pen this verse with the black ink of Time
That darkens life's page.
I sing this passive hymn in eternal rhyme
That is sung by every sage.

My pen trembles, my chaotic words flow not:
Am I bunked from thy grace?
Incarcerated in I, me, myself— all that is rot!
Set me free by thy embrace!

Thus I promise, and yet, I forget everyday!
For so oblivious am I!
Ineluctable debts of trifles have I yet to pay
Before the day I die!

I am born, O Dark Lord, to sing thy name,
But I've learnt only to shriek!
Like a seduced single man, I run after fame
Am I a poor poet or a freak?

# Remembering

our fallen soldiers of verse

*Janet Perkins Caldwell*

February 14, 1959 ~ September 20, 2016

*Alan W. Jankowski*

16 March 1961 ~ 10 March 2017

# Inner Child Press

# News

## Poetry Posse Members

We are so excited to share and announce a few of the current books, as well as the new and upcoming books of some of our Poetry Posse authors.

On the following pages we present to you ...

*Jackie Davis Allen*

*Gail Weston Shazor*

*hülya n. yılmaz*

*Nizar Sartawi*

*Faleeha Hassan*

*Fahredin Shehu*

*Caroline 'Ceri' Nazareno*

*Eliza Segiet*

*Teresa E. Gallion*

*William S. Peters, Sr.*

*Now Available*

*www.innerchildpress.com*

Fahredin Shehu
ORMUS

Now Available

www.innerchildpress.com

Ahead of My Time
. . . from the Streets to the Stages
Albert 'Infinite' Carrasco

Eliza Segiet
To Be More

## Now Available at

www.amazon.com/gp/product/B08MYL5B7S/ref=dbs_a_def_rwt_hsch_vapi_tkin_p1_i2

SEARCH FOR THE MAGICAL
MULTILINGUAL FROG
A Tale of Ribbit in 50 Languages
KIMBERLY BURNHAM

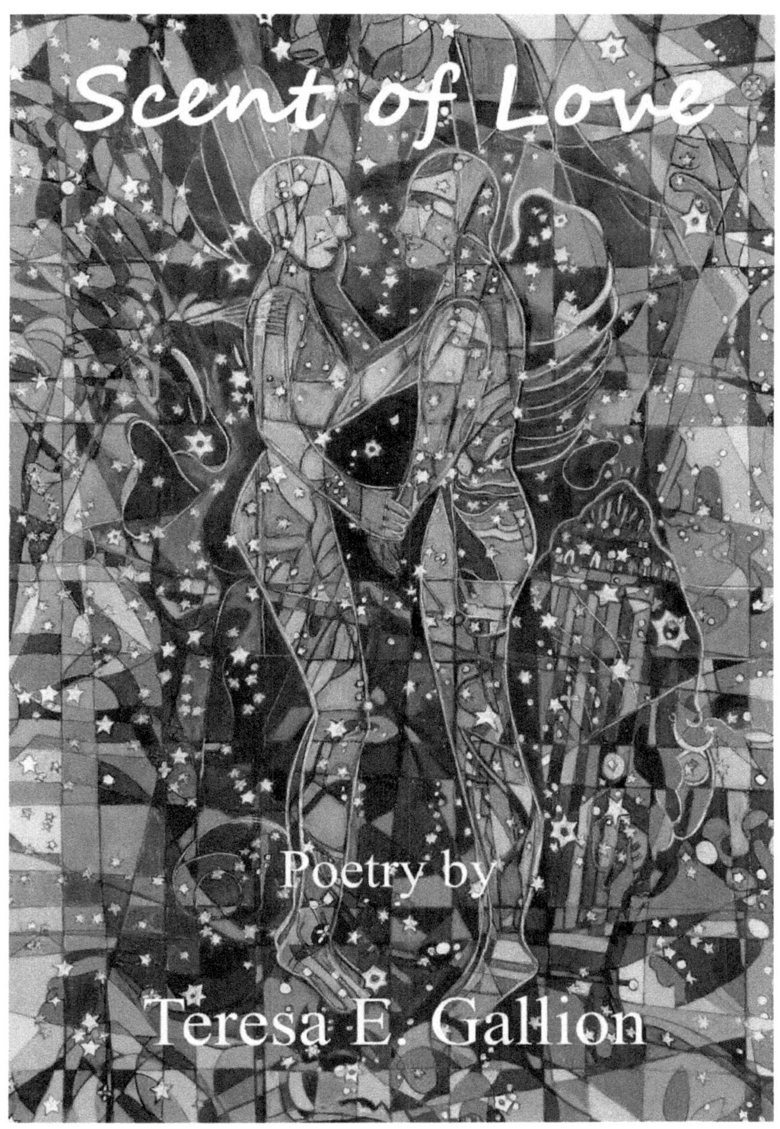
Scent of Love
Poetry by
Teresa E. Gallion

Now Available

www.innerchildpress.com

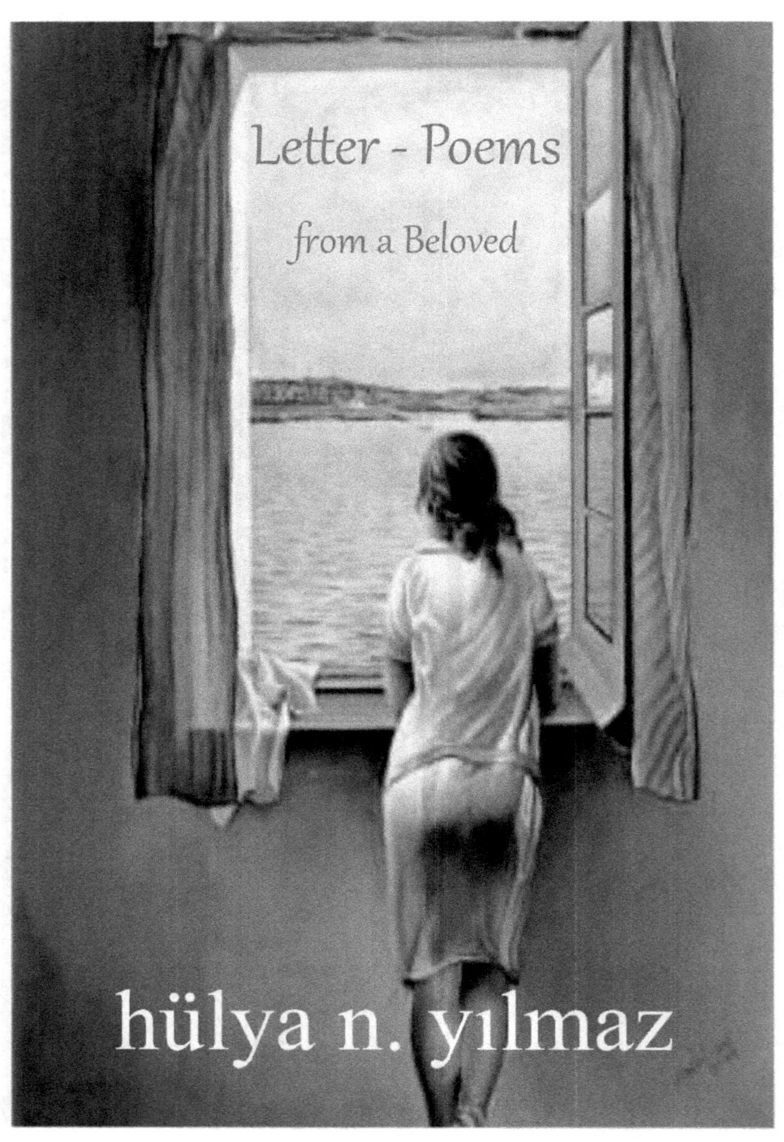
Letter - Poems
from a Beloved
hülya n. yılmaz

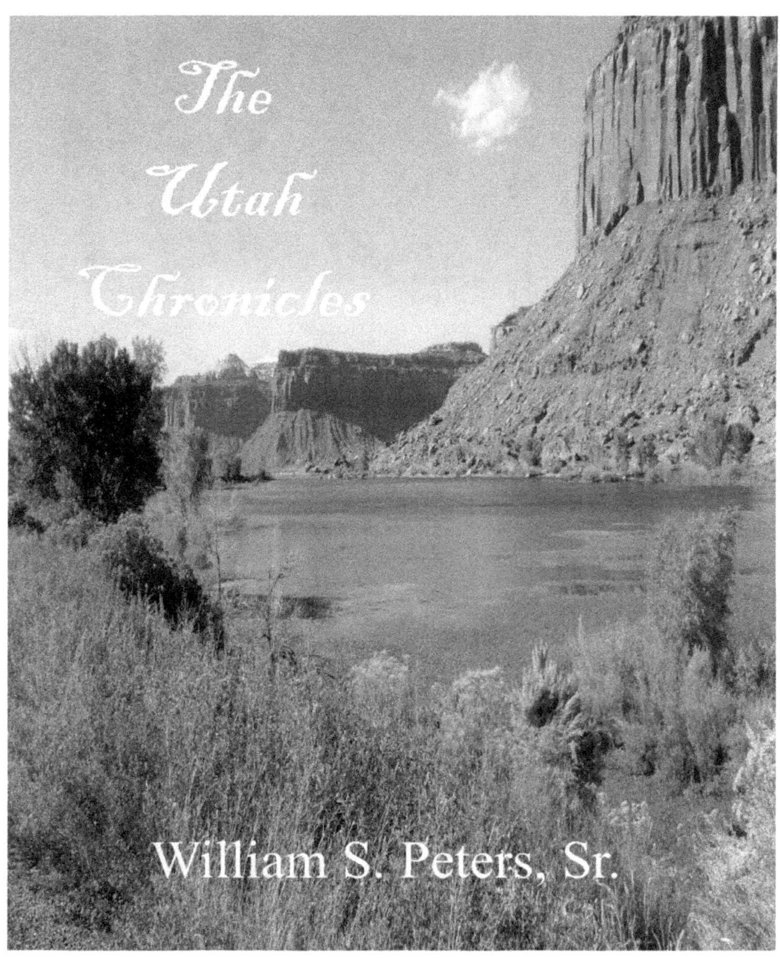
The Utah Chronicles
William S. Peters, Sr.

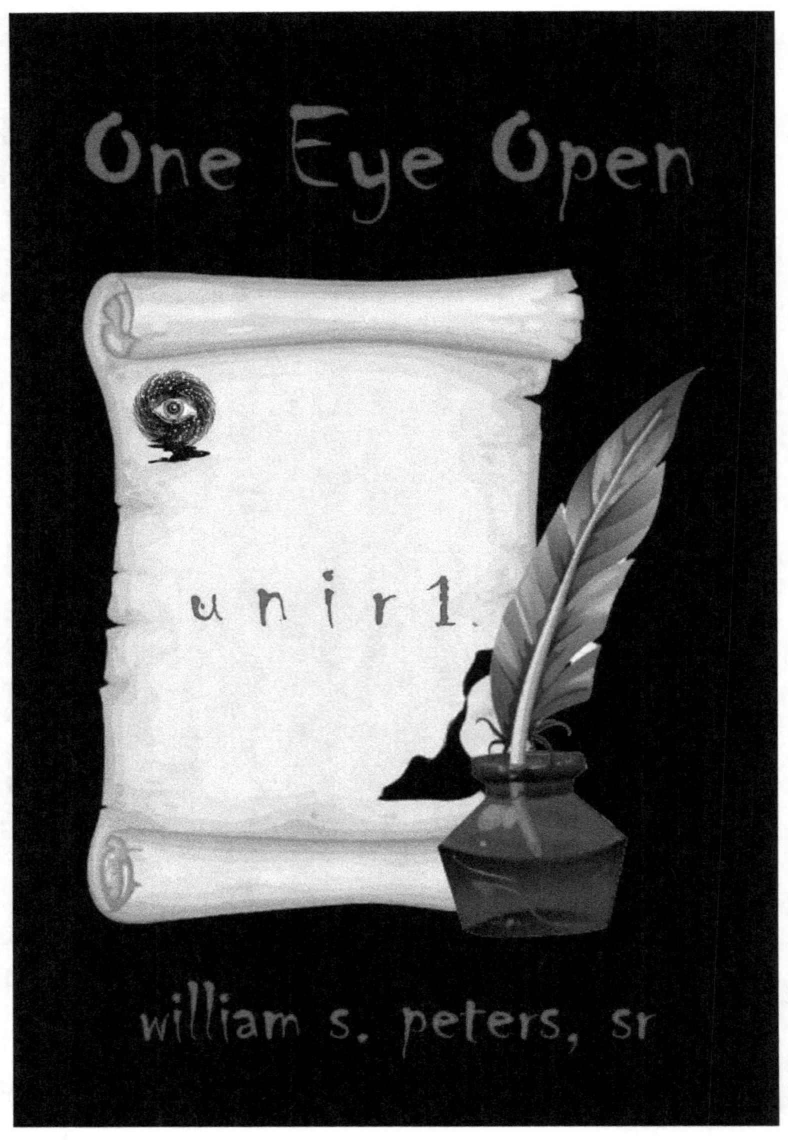
One Eye Open
unir1.
william s. peters, sr

*COMING SOON*

*www.innerchildpress.com*

The Book of krisar
volume v
william s. peters, sr.

## Now Available

www.innerchildpress.com

# The Book of krisar

Volume I

william s. peters, sr.

# The Book of krisar

Volume II

william s. peters, sr.

Now Available

www.innerchildpress.com

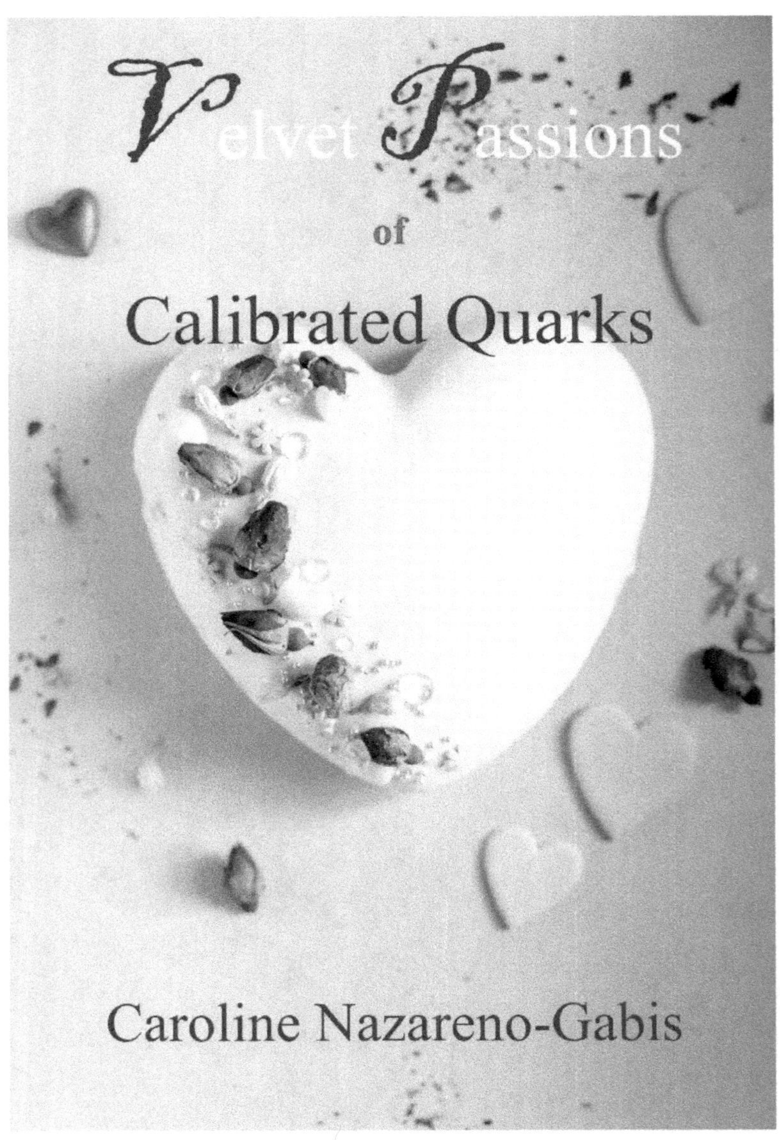
Velvet Passions
of
Calibrated Quarks
Caroline Nazareno-Gabis

*Now Available*

*www.innerchildpress.com*

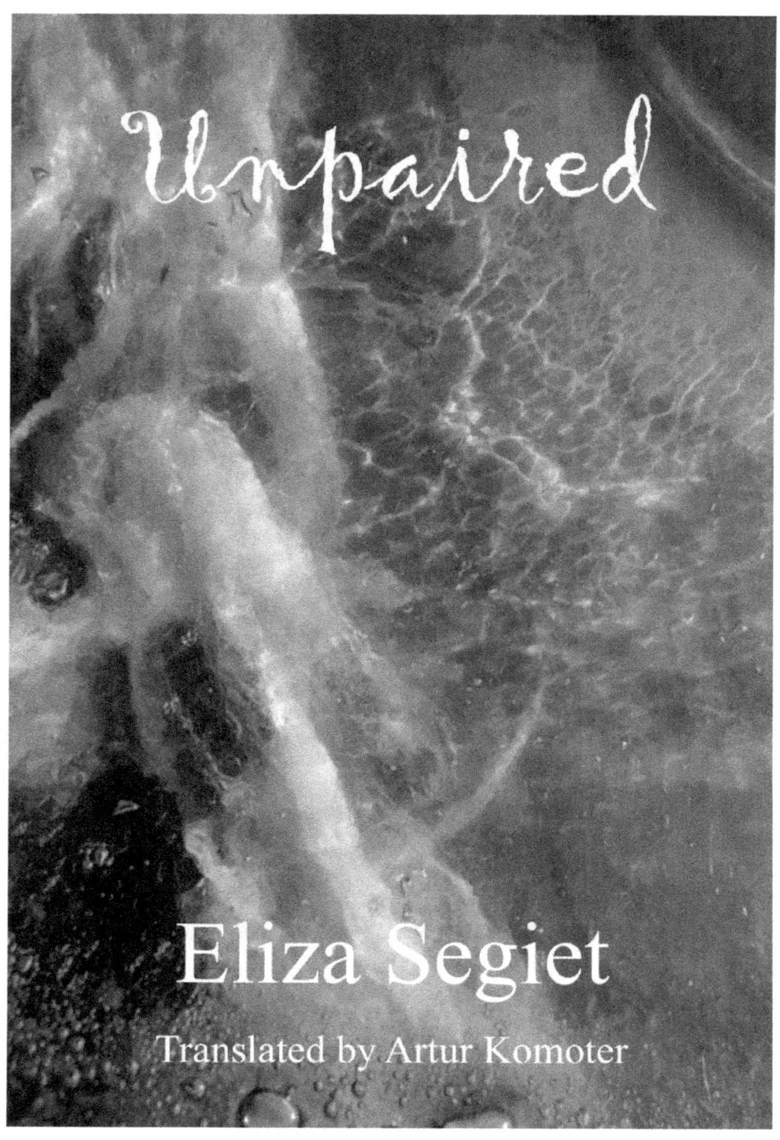
Unpaired
Eliza Segiet
Translated by Artur Komoter

Private Issue

www.innerchildpress.com

Canlarım
My Lifeblood
poetry in Turkish and English
hülya n. yılmaz

Butterfly's Voice
Faleeha Hassan
Translated by William M. Hutchins

Now Available at

www.innerchildpress.com

No Illusions
Through the Looking Glass
J.D.ALLEN /72
Jackie Davis Allen

*Now Available at*

*www.innerchildpress.com*

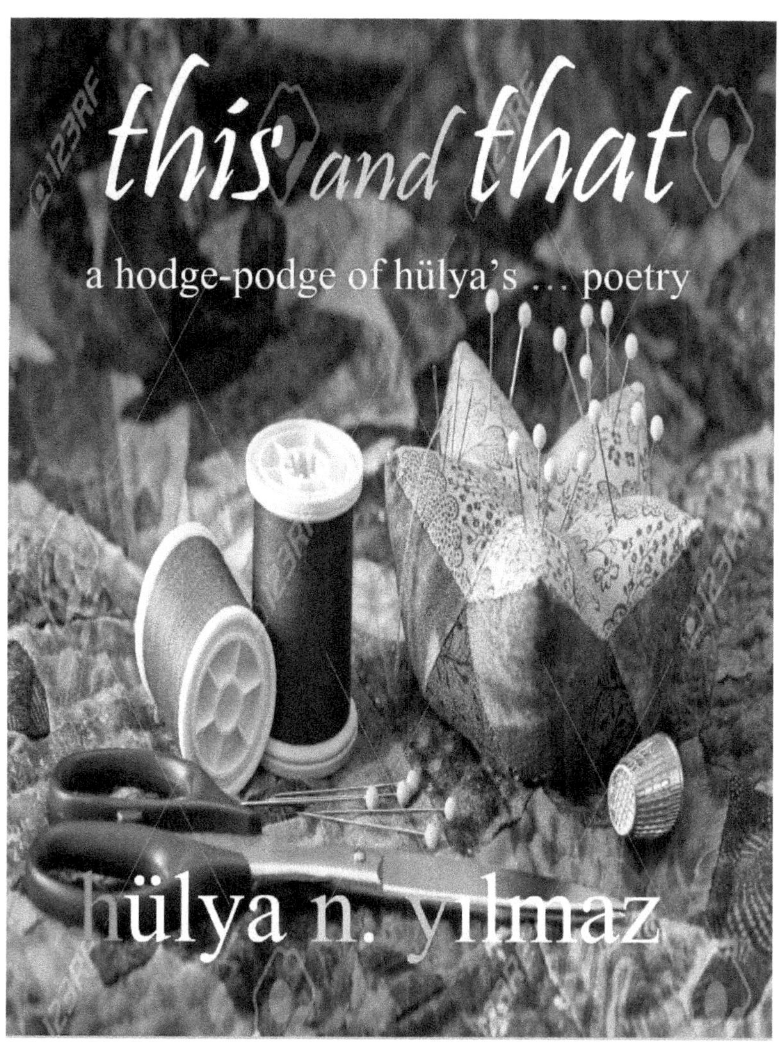
this and that
a hodge-podge of hülya's … poetry
hülya n. yılmaz

Now Available at

www.innerchildpress.com

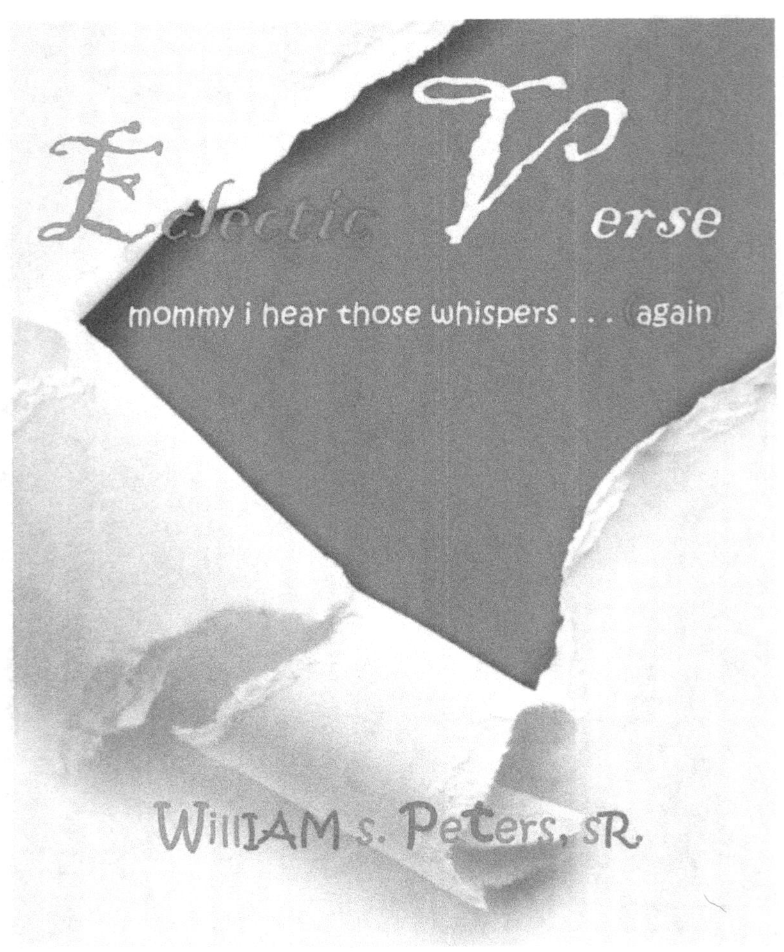
Eclectic Verse
mommy i hear those whispers . . . (again)
WillIAM s. Peters, sR

*Now Available at*

*www.innerchildpress.com*

# HERENOW

FAHREDIN SHEHU

Now Available at

www.innerchildpress.com

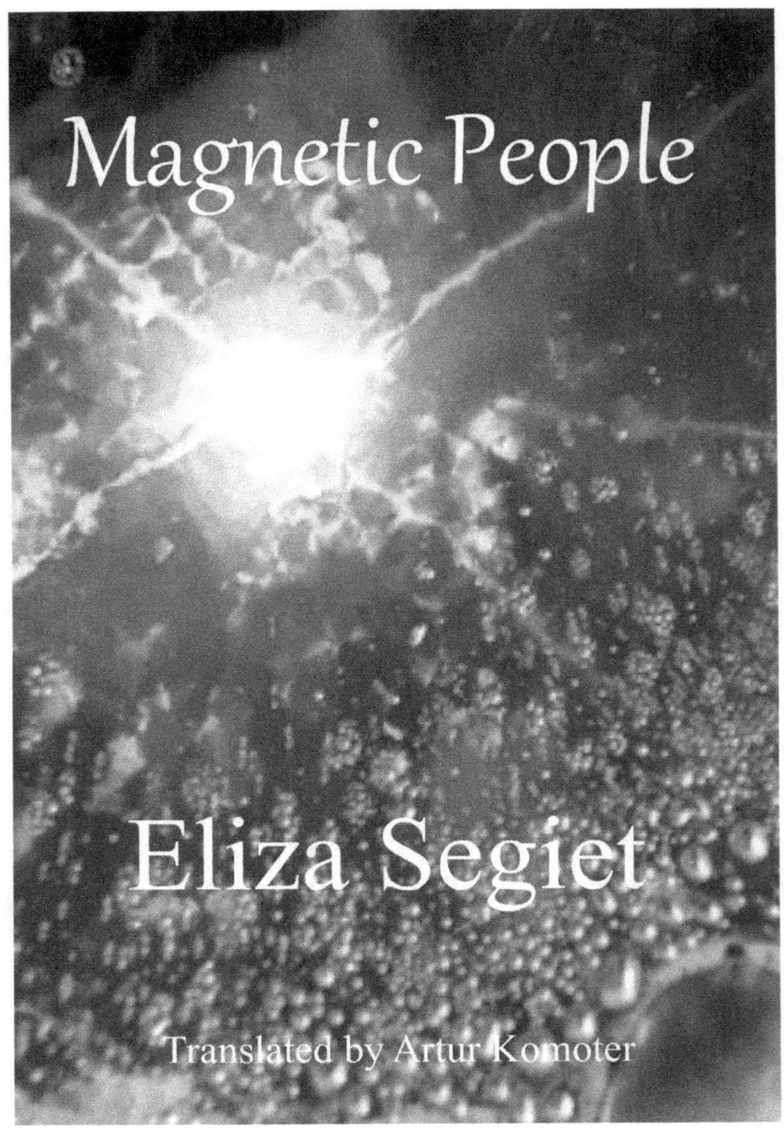
Magnetic People
Eliza Segiet
Translated by Artur Komoter

*Now Available at*

*www.innerchildpress.com*

Dark Side
of the
Moon
Jackie Davis Allen

Now Available at

www.innerchildpress.com

Lies
My
Grandfathers
Told
Me
Gail Weston Shazor

Aflame
Memoirs in Verse
hülya n. yılmaz

Now Available at

www.innerchildpress.com

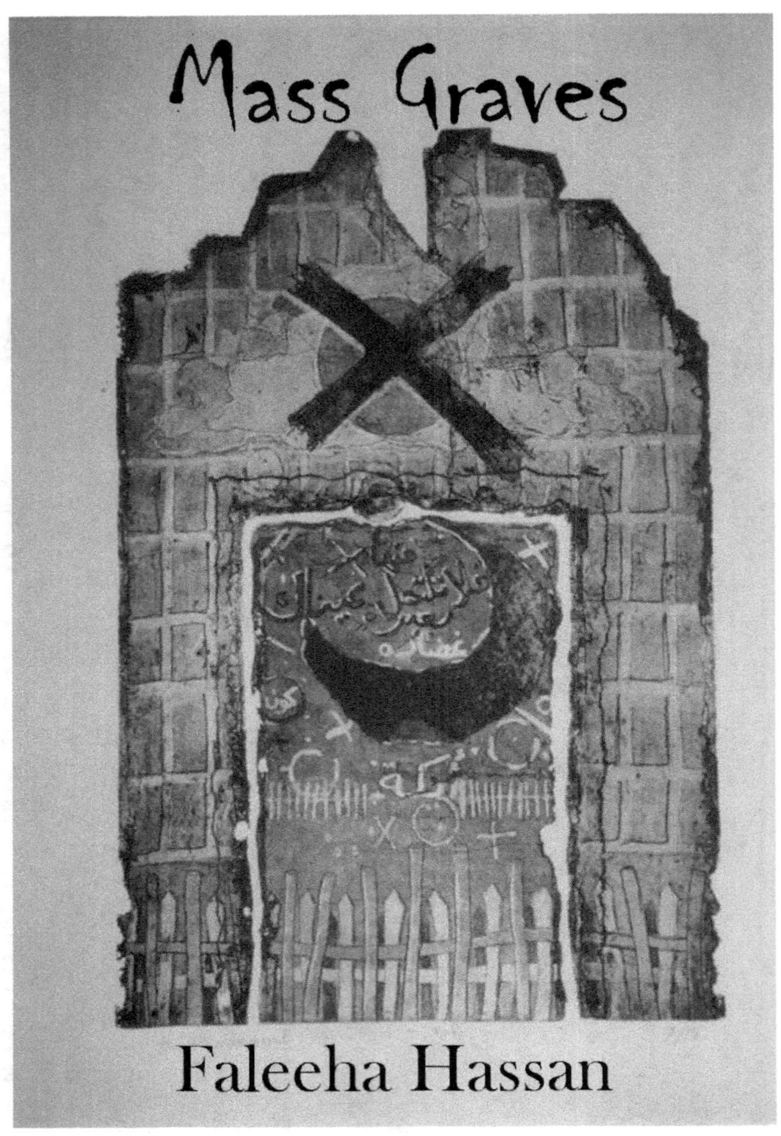
Mass Graves
Faleeha Hassan

Now Available at

www.innerchildpress.com

Now Available at

www.innerchildpress.com

7 Days
in
Palestine
william s. peters sr.

*Now Available at*

*www.innerchildpress.com*

inner child press

presents

Tunisia My Love

william s. peters, sr.

Now Available at

www.innerchildpress.com

INNER CHILD PRESS
THIS IS WHY I
SLEEP
william s. peters sr.

*Now Available at*

*www.innerchildpress.com*

Other

Anthological

works from

Inner Child Press International

www.innerchildpress.com

# World Healing World Peace 2020

## Poets for Humanity

*Now Available*

www.worldhealingworldpeacepoetry.com

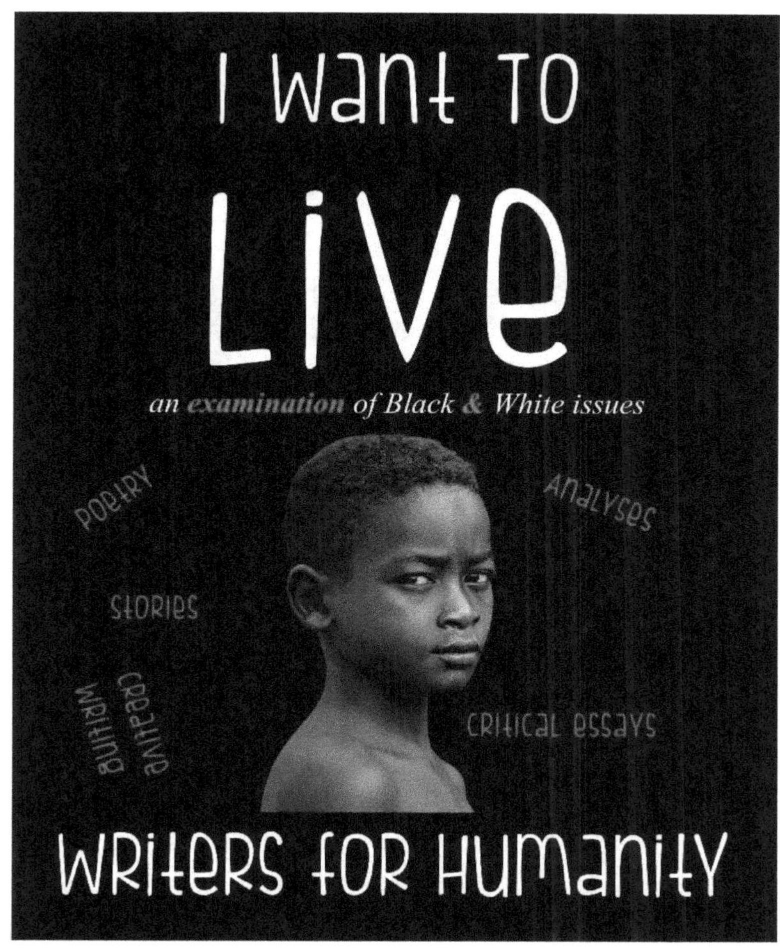
I Want To
Live
an examination of Black & White issues
Poetry
Analyses
Stories
Creative Writing
Critical essays
Writers for Humanity

Now Available

www.innerchildpress.com

Inner Child Press International
&
The Year of the Poet
**present**

# Poetry

*the best of 2020*

*Poets of the World*

*Now Available*

*www.innerchildpress.com*

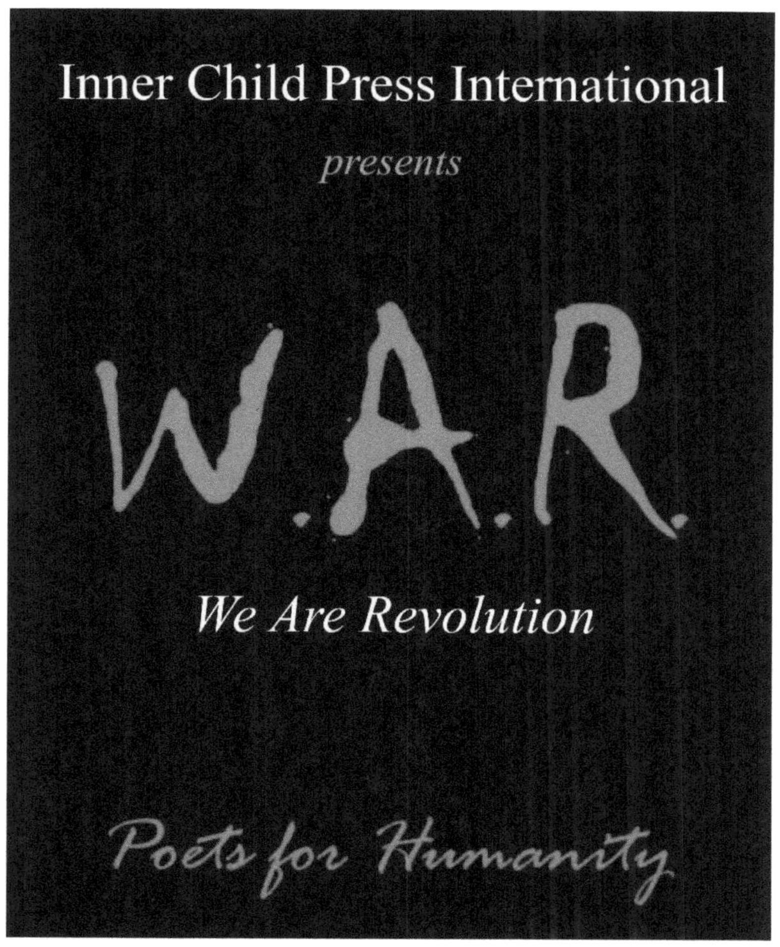
Inner Child Press International
presents
W.A.R.
We Are Revolution
Poets for Humanity

Now Available

www.innerchildpress.com

Corona
Social Distancing
Poets for Humanity

Poetry
from the
Balkans
The Balkan Poets

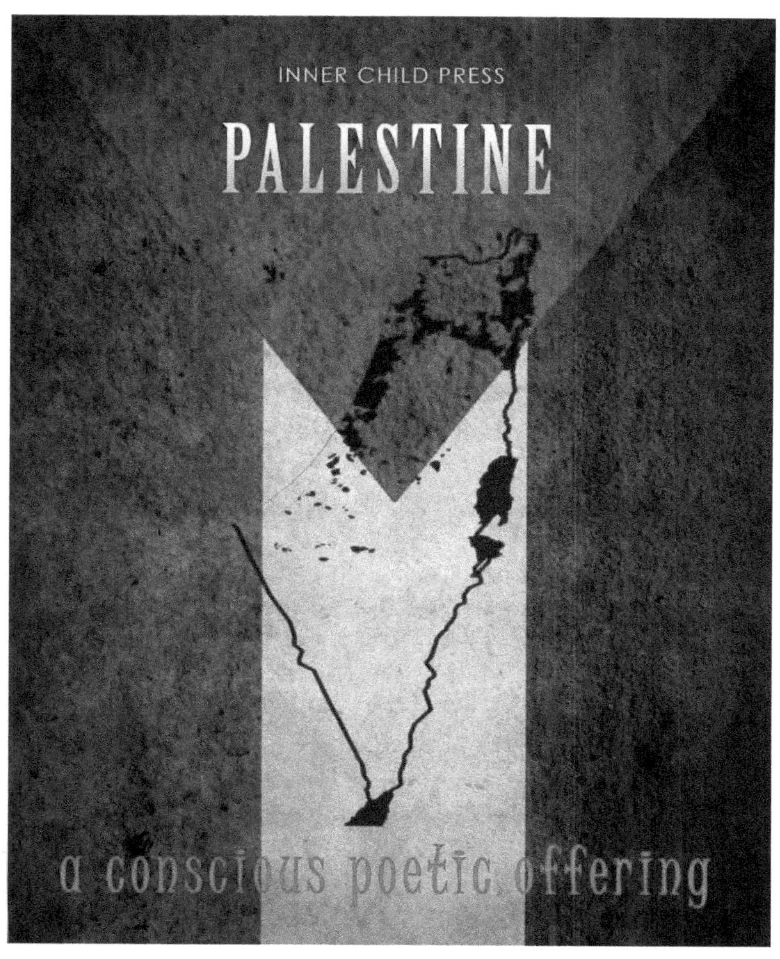
INNER CHILD PRESS
PALESTINE
a conscious poetic offering

INNER CHILD PRESS
WORLD HEALING
WORLD PEACE
2018
A Poetry Anthology for Humanity

Inner Child Press International

presents

# A Love Anthology

2019

The Love Poets

INNER CHILD PRESS
WORLD HEALING
WORLD PEACE
2018
A Poetry Anthology for Humanity

Now Available

www.worldhealingworldpeacepoetry.com

INNER CHILD PRESS
World Healing
World Peace
A Poetry Anthology 2014
Volume 1
INNER CHILD PRESS
World Healing
World Peace
A Poetry Anthology 2014
Volume 2

World Healing
World Peace
2012
A POETRY ANTHOLOGY
Volume 1
World Healing
World Peace
2012
A POETRY ANTHOLOGY
Volume 2

Now Available

www.worldhealingworldpeacepoetry.com

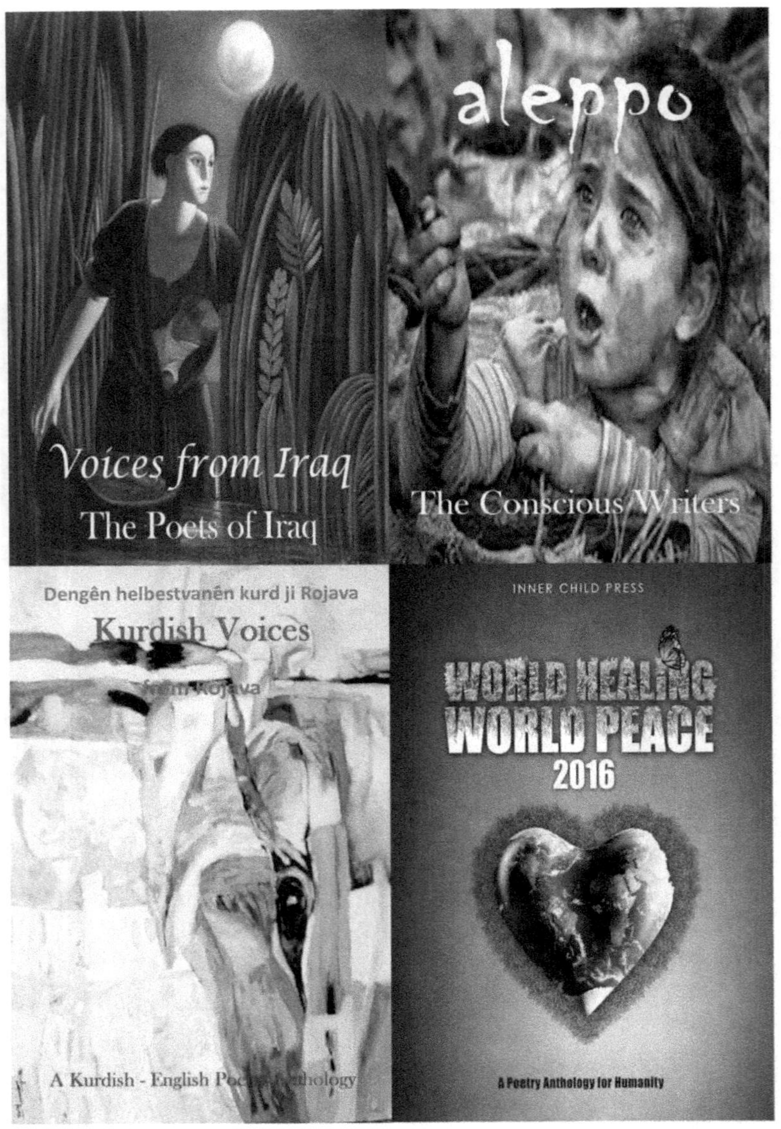
Voices from Iraq
The Poets of Iraq
aleppo
The Conscious Writers
Dengên helbestvanên kurd ji Rojava
Kurdish Voices
A Kurdish - English Poetry Anthology
INNER CHILD PRESS
WORLD HEALING
WORLD PEACE
2016
A Poetry Anthology for Humanity

Now Available

www.innerchildpress.com/anthologies

Mandela

The Man

His Life

Its Meaning

Our Words

Poetry . . . Commentary & Stories

*The Anthological Writers*

A GATHERING OF WORDS

POETRY & COMMENTARY

FOR

TRAYVON MARTIN

INNER CHILD PRESS
BLACK MALE-D
The Black Male Writers
with words from Imam Jamil Abdullah Al-Amin
aka H. Rap Brown

I want my poetry to . . . volume 4

the conscious poets

*inspired by* . . . Monte Smith

Now Available

www.innerchildpress.com/anthologies

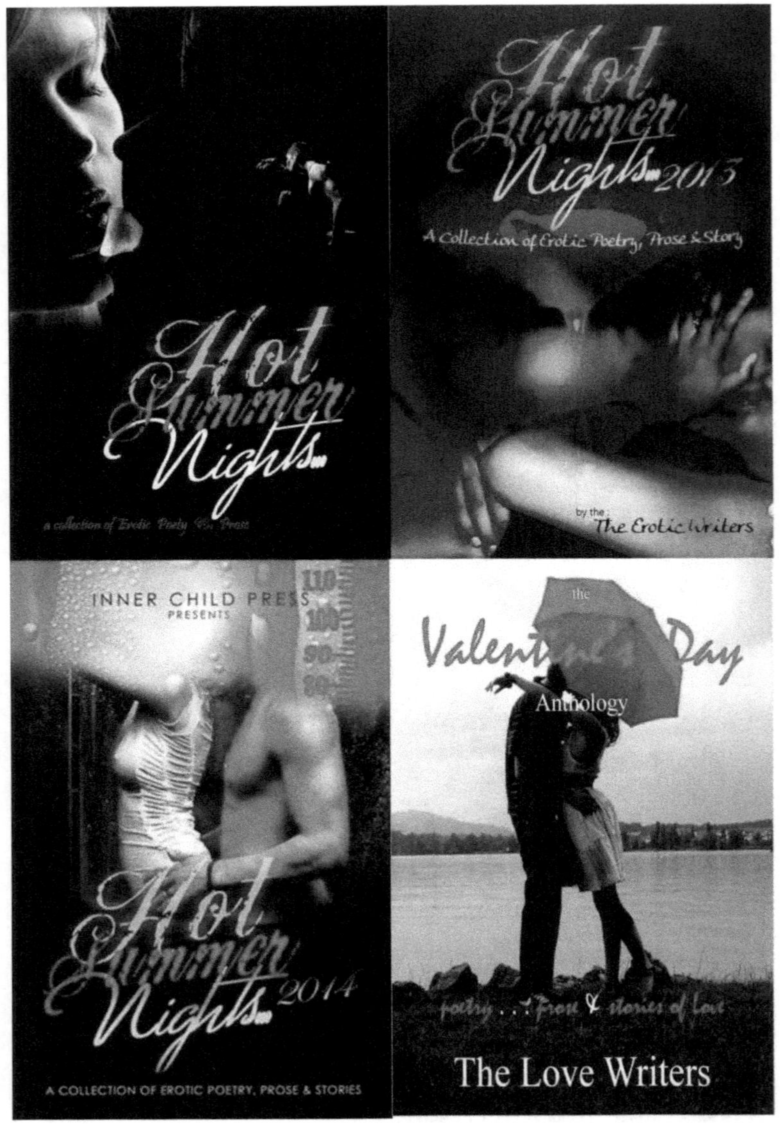
Hot Summer Nights...
Hot Summer Nights...2013
A Collection of Erotic Poetry, Prose & Story
by the The Erotic Writers
INNER CHILD PRESS
PRESENTS
Hot Summer Nights...2014
A COLLECTION OF EROTIC POETRY, PROSE & STORIES
the
Anthology
The Love Writers

Now Available

www.innerchildpress.com/anthologies

# Inner Child Press Anthologies

Janet
gone too soon . . .
healing through words
Poetry ... Prose ... Prayer ... Stories
a
Poetically
Spoken
Anthology
volume I
Collector's Edition
The Poetry Posse
Presents
an anthology
of
Love
The Poetry Posse 2016

## Now Available

www.innerchildpress.com/anthologies

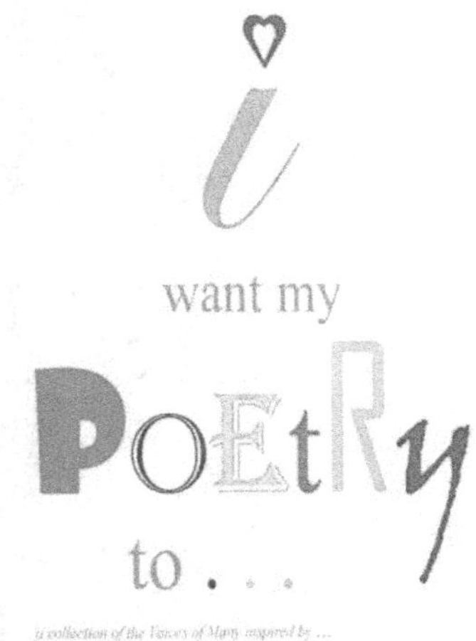
want my
PoEtRy
to . . .
a collection of the Voices of Many inspired by ...
Monte Smith

a collection of the Voices of Many inspired by ...
Monte Smith
want my

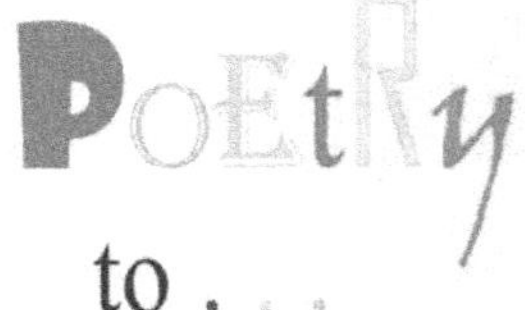
PoEtRy
to . . .

volume II

want
my
Poetry
to . . .
volume 3
a collection of the Voices of Many inspired by . . .

Monte Smith

11 Words

( 9 lines . . . )

*for those who are challenged*

Poetry Dancer

**Now Available**

www.innerchildpress.com/anthologies

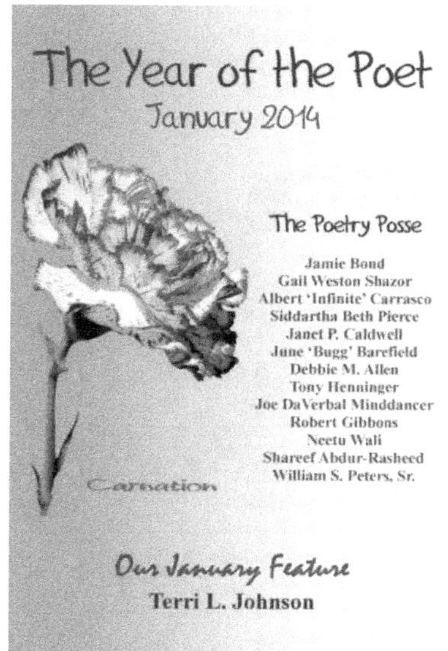
The Year of the Poet
January 2014
The Poetry Posse
Jamie Bond
Gail Weston Shazor
Albert 'Infinite' Carrasco
Siddartha Beth Pierce
Janet P. Caldwell
June 'Bugg' Barefield
Debbie M. Allen
Tony Henninger
Joe DaVerbal Minddancer
Robert Gibbons
Neetu Wali
Shareef Abdur-Rasheed
William S. Peters, Sr.
Carnation
Our January Feature
Terri L. Johnson

the Year of the Poet
February 2014
violets
The Poetry Posse
Our February Features
Teresa E. Gallion & Robert Gibson

the Year of the Poet

March 2014

The Poetry Posse

Jamie Bond
Gail Weston Shazor
Albert 'Infinite' Carrasco
Siddartha Beth Pierce
Janet P. Caldwell
June 'Bugg' Barefield
Debbie M. Allen
Tony Henninger
Joe DaVerbal Minddancer
Robert Gibbons
Neetu Wali
Shareef Abdur-Rasheed
Kimberly Burnham
William S. Peters, Sr.

daffodil

Our March Featured Poets

Alicia C. Cooper & hülya yılmaz

the Year of the Poet
April 2014
The Poetry Posse
Our April Featured Poets
Fahredin Shehu
Martina Reisz Newberry
Justin Blackburn
Monte Smith
Sweet Pea
celebrating international poetry month

## Now Available

www.innerchildpress.com/the-year-of-the-poet

the year of the poet
May 2014
May's Featured Poets
ReeCee
Joski the Poet
Shannon Stanton
Dedicated To our Children
The Poetry Posse
Lily of the Valley
the Year of the Poet
June 2014
Love & Relationship
Rose
June's Featured Poets
Shantelle McLin
Jacqueline D. E. Kennedy
Abraham N. Benjamin
The Poetry Posse
Jamie Bond
Gail Weston Shazor
Albert 'Infinite' Carrasco
Siddartha Beth Pierce
Janet P. Caldwell
June 'Bugg' Barefield
Debbie M. Allen
Tony Henninger
Joe DaVerbal Minddancer
Robert Gibbons
Neetu Wali
Shareef Abdur-Rasheed
Kimberly Burnham
William S. Peters, Sr.
The Year of the Poet
July 2014
July Feature Poets
Christena A. V. Williams
Dr. John R. Strum
Kolade Olanrewaju Freedom
The Poetry Posse
Lotus
Asian Flower of the Month
The Year of the Poet
August 2014
Gladiolus
The Poetry Posse
August Feature Poets
Ann White * Rosalind Cherry * Sheila Jenkins

# Now Available

www.innerchildpress.com/the-year-of-the-poet

The Year of the Poet
September 2014
Aster
Morning-Glory
September Feature Poets

THE YEAR OF THE POET
October 2014
Red Poppy
The Poetry Posse
October Feature Poets
Ceri Naz * RaJendra Padhi * Elizabeth Castillo

THE YEAR OF THE POET
November 2014
Chrysanthemum
The Poetry Posse
November Feature Poets

THE YEAR OF THE POET
December 2014
Narcissus

**Now Available**

www.innerchildpress.com/the-year-of-the-poet

# Inner Child Press Anthologies

The Year of the Poet II
May 2015
May's Featured Poets
Geri Algeri
Emeralds
The Poetry Posse 2015
Siddartha Beth Pierce * Janet P. Caldwell * Tony Henninger
Joe DaVerbal Minddancer * Neetu Wali * Shareef Abdur – Rasheed
Kimberly Burnham * Ann White * Keith Alan Hamilton
Katherine Wyatt * Fahredin Shehu * Hülya N. Yılmaz
Teresa E. Gallion * Jackie Allen * William S. Peters, Sr.


## The Year of the Poet II

**June 2015**

June's Featured Poets

Anahit Arustamyan * Yvette D. Murrell * Renato A. Walker

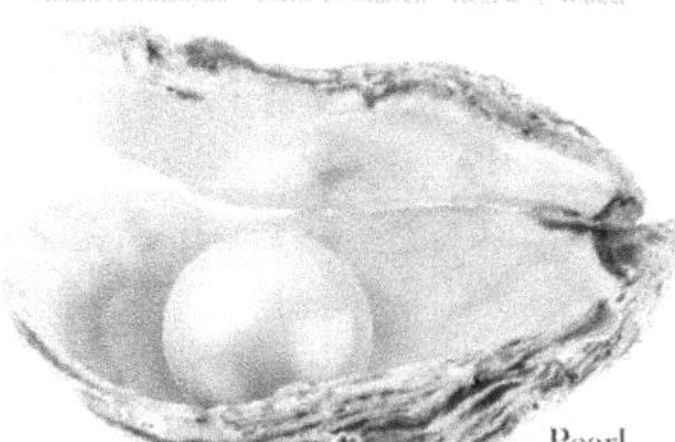

Pearl

The Poetry Posse 2015

Jamie Bond * Gail Weston Shazor * Albert 'Infinite' Carrasco
Siddartha Beth Pierce * Janet P. Caldwell * Tony Henninger
Joe DaVerbal Minddancer * Neetu Wali * Shareef Abdur – Rasheed
Kimberly Burnham * Ann White * Keith Alan Hamilton
Katherine Wyatt * Fahredin Shehu * Hülya N. Yılmaz
Teresa E. Gallion * Jackie Allen * William S. Peters, Sr

## The Year of the Poet II

**July 2015**

The Featured Poets for July 2015

Abhik Shome * Christina Neal * Robert Neal

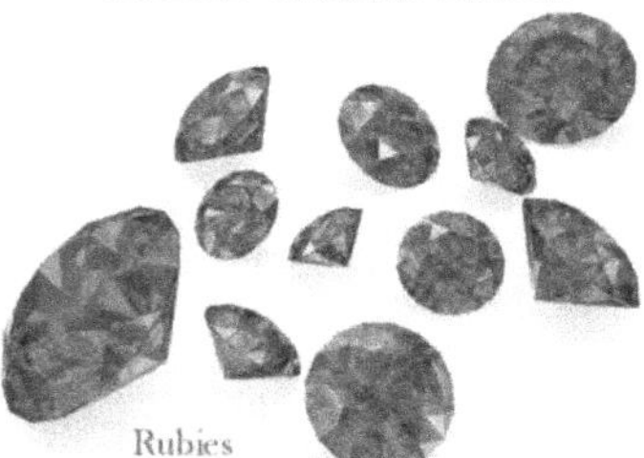

Rubies

The Poetry Posse 2015

Jamie Bond * Gail Weston Shazor * Albert 'Infinite' Carrasco
Siddartha Beth Pierce * Janet P. Caldwell * Tony Henninger
Joe DaVerbal Minddancer * Neetu Wali * Shareef Abdur – Rasheed
Kimberly Burnham * Ann White * Keith Alan Hamilton
Katherine Wyatt * Fahredin Shehu * Hülya N. Yılmaz
Teresa E. Gallion * Jackie Allen * William S. Peters, Sr

## The Year of the Poet II

**August 2015**

Peridot

Featured Poets

Gayle Howell
Ann Chalasz
Christopher Schultz

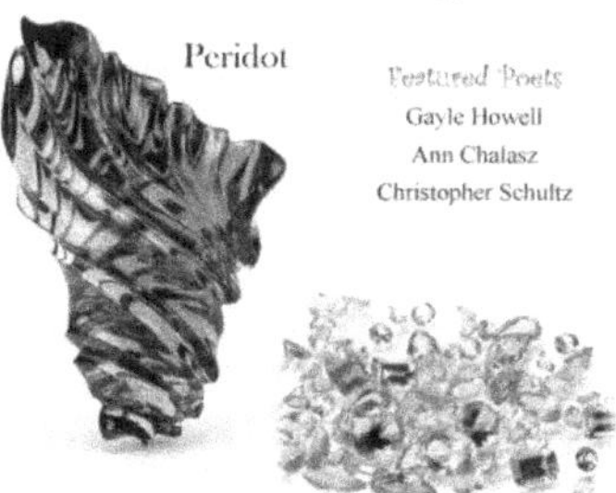

The Poetry Posse 2015

Jamie Bond * Gail Weston Shazor * Albert 'Infinite' Carrasco
Siddartha Beth Pierce * Janet P. Caldwell * Tony Henninger
Joe DaVerbal Minddancer * Neetu Wali * Shareef Abdur – Rasheed
Kimberly Burnham * Ann White * Keith Alan Hamilton
Katherine Wyatt * Fahredin Shehu * Hülya N. Yılmaz
Teresa E. Gallion * Jackie Allen * William S. Peters, Sr

## Now Available

www.innerchildpress.com/the-year-of-the-poet

The Year of the Poet II
Featured Poets
Alfreda Ghee   Lonneice Weeks Badley   Demetrios Trifiatis
Sapphires
Jamie Bond * Gail Weston Shazor * Albert 'Infinite' Carrasco
Siddartha Beth Pierce * Janet P. Caldwell * Tony Henninger
Joe DaVerbal Minddancer * Neetu Wali * Shareef Abdur – Rasheed
Kimberly Burnham * Ann White * Keith Alan Hamilton
Katherine Wyatt * Fahredin Shehu * Hülya N. Yılmaz
Teresa E. Gallion * Jackie Allen * William S. Peters, Sr.
The Year of the Poet II
October 2015
Featured Poets
Monte Smith * Laura J. Wolfe * William Washington
Opal
The Poetry Posse 2015
Jamie Bond * Gail Weston Shazor * Albert 'Infinite' Carrasco
Siddartha Beth Pierce * Janet P. Caldwell * Tony Henninger
Joe DaVerbal Minddancer * Neetu Wali * Shareef Abdur – Rasheed
Kimberly Burnham * Ann White * Keith Alan Hamilton
Katherine Wyatt * Fahredin Shehu * Hülya N. Yılmaz
Teresa E. Gallion * Jackie Allen * William S. Peters, Sr.

The Year of the Poet II
November 2015
Featured Poets
Topaz
The Poetry Posse 2015
Jamie Bond * Gail Weston Shazor * Albert 'Infinite' Carrasco
Siddartha Beth Pierce * Janet P. Caldwell * Tony Henninger
Joe DaVerbal Minddancer * Neetu Wali * Shareef Abdur – Rasheed
Kimberly Burnham * Ann White * Keith Alan Hamilton
Katherine Wyatt * Fahredin Shehu * Hülya N. Yılmaz
Teresa E. Gallion * Jackie Allen * William S. Peters, Sr.

The Year of the Poet II
December 2015

Featured Poets
Kerione Bryan * Michelle Joan Barulich * Neville Hiatt

Turquoise

The Poetry Posse 2015
Jamie Bond * Gail Weston Shazor * Albert 'Infinite' Carrasco
Siddartha Beth Pierce * Janet P. Caldwell * Tony Henninger
Joe DaVerbal Minddancer * Neetu Wali * Shareef Abdur – Rasheed
Kimberly Burnham * Ann White * Keith Alan Hamilton
Katherine Wyatt * Fahredin Shehu * Hülya N. Yılmaz
Teresa E. Gallion * Jackie Allen * William S. Peters, Sr.

## Now Available

www.innerchildpress.com/the-year-of-the-poet

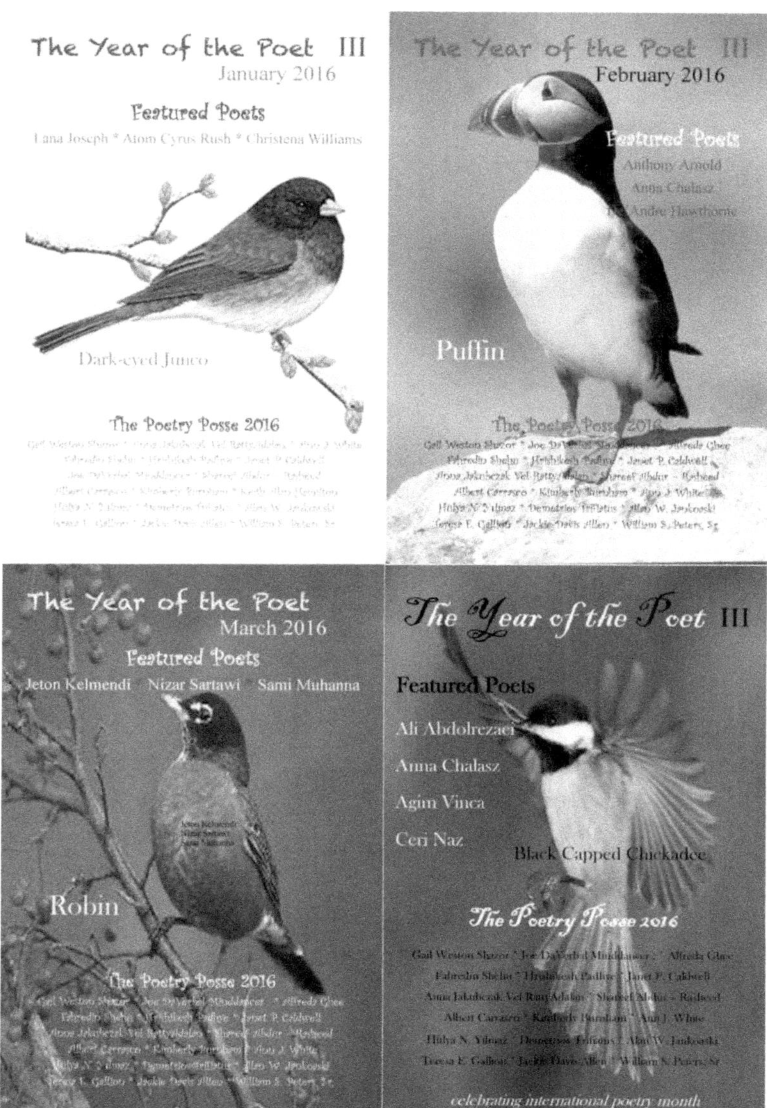
The Year of the Poet III
January 2016
Featured Poets
Lana Joseph * Atom Cyrus Rush * Christena Williams
Dark-eyed Junco
The Poetry Posse 2016
The Year of the Poet III
February 2016
Featured Poets
Anthony Arnold
Anna Chalasz
Andre Hawthorne
Puffin
The Poetry Posse 2016
The Year of the Poet
March 2016
Featured Poets
Jeton Kelmendi * Nizar Sartawi * Sami Muhanna
Robin
The Poetry Posse 2016
The Year of the Poet III
Featured Poets
Ali Abdolrezaei
Anna Chalasz
Agim Vinca
Ceri Naz
Black Capped Chickadee
The Poetry Posse 2016
celebrating international poetry month

## Now Available

www.innerchildpress.com/the-year-of-the-poet

Inner Child Press Anthologies

The Year of the Poet
May 2016
Bob Strum
Barbara Allan
D.L. Davis
Oriole
The Year of the Poet III
June 2016
Featured Poets
Qibrije Demiri- Frangu
Naime Beqiraj
Faleeha Hassan
Bedri Zyberaj
Black Necked Stilt
The Poetry Posse 2016
Iram Fatima 'Ashi'
Langley Shazor
Jody Doty
Emilia T. Davis
Indigo Bunting
The Poetry Posse 2016
The Year of the Poet III
August 2016
Featured Poets
Anita Dash
Irena Jovanovic
Malgorzata Gouluda
Painted Bunting
The Poetry Posse 2016

Now Available

www.innerchildpress.com/the-year-of-the-poet

Featured Poets
Long Billed Curle
The Year of the Poet III
October 2016
Featured Poets
The Year of the Poet III
November 2016
Featured Poets
Rosemary Burns
Robin Ouzman Hislop
Northern Cardinal
The Poetry Posse 2016
the Poet III
December 2016
Featured Poets
Samih Masoud
Mountassir Aziz Bien
Abdulkadir Musa
Rough Legged Hawk
The Poetry Posse 2016

Now Available

www.innerchildpress.com/the-year-of-the-poet

The Year of the Poet IV
Quaking Aspen
The Poetry Posse 2017

The Year of the Poet IV
February 2017
Featured Poets
Lin Ross
Witch Hazel
The Poetry Posse 2017

The Year of the Poet IV
March 2017
Featured Poets
Tremell Stevens
The Eastern Redbud
The Poetry Posse 2017

The Year of the Poet IV
April 2017
Featured Poets
The Blossoming Cherry
The Poetry Posse 2017

## Now Available

www.innerchildpress.com/the-year-of-the-poet

# Inner Child Press Anthologies

The Year of the Poet IV
May 2017
The Flowering Dogwood Tree

Featured Poets
Kallisa Powell
Alicja Maria Kuberska
Fethi Sassi

The Poetry Posse 2017

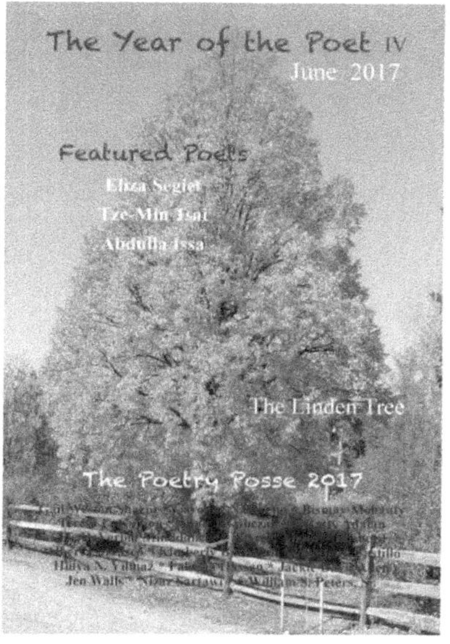
The Year of the Poet IV
June 2017
Featured Poets
Eliza Segiet
Tze-Min Tsai
Abdulla Issa
The Linden Tree
The Poetry Posse 2017

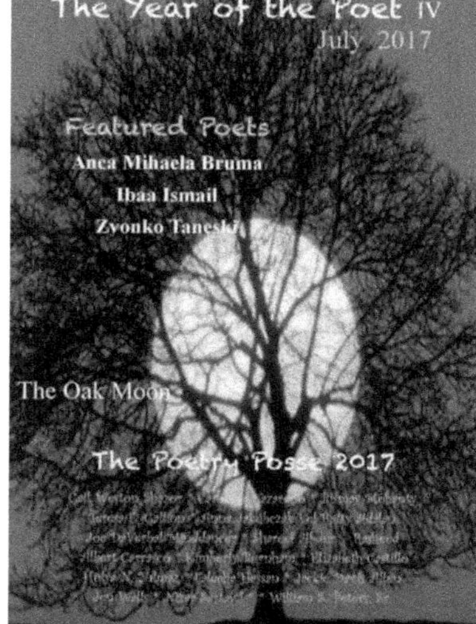
The Year of the Poet IV
July 2017
Featured Poets
Anca Mihaela Bruma
Ibaa Ismail
Zvonko Taneski
The Oak Moon
The Poetry Posse 2017

The Year of the Poet IV
August 2017

Jonathan Aquino
Kitty Hsu
Langley Shazor
The Hazelnut Tree

The Poetry Posse 2017

## Now Available

www.innerchildpress.com/the-year-of-the-poet

# Inner Child Press Anthologies

The Year of the Poet IV
September 2017

Featured Poets
**Martina Reisz Newberry**
**Ameer Nassir**
**Christine Fulco Neal**
**Robert Neal**

The Elm Tree

The Poetry Posse 2017

Gail Weston Shazor * Caroline Nazareno * Bismay Mohanty
Teresa E. Gallion * Anna Jakubczak Vel Ratty Adalan
Joe DaVerbal Minddancer * Shareef Abdur – Rasheed
Albert Carrasco * Kimberly Burnham * Elizabeth Castillo
Hülya N. Yılmaz * Faleeha Hassan * Jackie Davis Allen
Jen Walls * Nizar Sartawi * * William S. Peters, Sr.

The Year of the Poet IV
October 2017

Featured Poets
**Ahmed Abu Saleem**
**Nedal Al-Qaeim**
**Sadeddin Shahin**

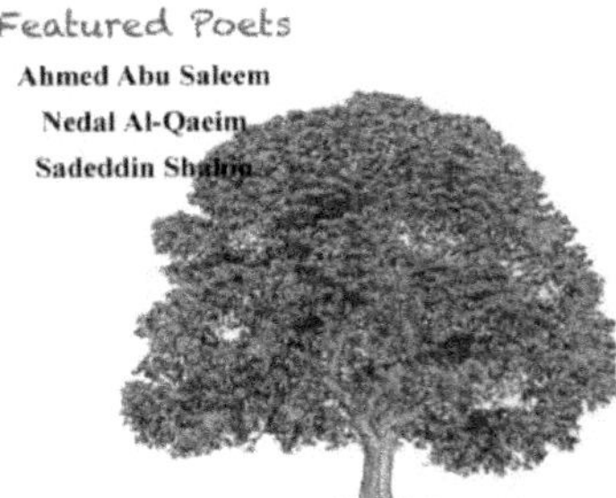

The Black Walnut Tree

**The Poetry Posse 2017**

Gail Weston Shazor * Caroline Nazareno * Bismay Mohanty
Teresa E. Gallion * Anna Jakubczak Vel Ratty Adalan
Joe DaVerbal Minddancer * Shareef Abdur – Rasheed
Albert Carrasco * Kimberly Burnham * Elizabeth Castillo
Hülya N. Yılmaz * Faleeha Hassan * Jackie Davis Allen
Jen Walls * Nizar Sartawi * * William S. Peters, Sr.

The Year of the Poet IV
November 2017

Featured Poets
Kay Peters
Alfreda D. Ghee
Gabriella Garofalo
Rosemary Cappello

The Tree of Life

The Poetry Posse 2017

Gail Weston Shazor * Caroline Nazareno * Bismay Mohanty
Teresa E. Gallion * Anna Jakubczak Vel Ratty Adalan
Joe DaVerbal Minddancer * Shareef Abdur – Rasheed
Albert Carrasco * Kimberly Burnham * Elizabeth Castillo
Hülya N. Yılmaz * Faleeha Hassan * Jackie Davis Allen
Jen Walls * Nizar Sartawi * William S. Peters, Sr.

The Year of the Poet IV
December 2017

Featured Poets
Justice Clarke
Mariel M. Pabroa
Kiley Brown

The Fig Tree

The Poetry Posse 2017

Gail Weston Shazor * Caroline Nazareno * Bismay Mohanty
Teresa E. Gallion * Anna Jakubczak Vel Ratty Adalan
Joe DaVerbal Minddancer * Shareef Abdur – Rasheed
Albert Carrasco * Kimberly Burnham * Elizabeth Castillo
Hülya N. Yılmaz * Faleeha Hassan * Jackie Davis Allen
Jen Walls * Nizar Sartawi * William S. Peters, Sr.

## Now Available

www.innerchildpress.com/the-year-of-the-poet

The Year of the Poet V
January 2018
Featured Poets
Iyad Shamasnah
Yasmeen Hamzeh
Ali Abdolrezaei
Aksum
The Poetry Posse 2018
The Year of the Poet V
February 2018
Sabean
Featured Poets
Muhammad Azram
Anna Szawracka
Abhilipsa Kuanar
Aanika Aery
The Poetry Posse 2018
Gail Weston Shazor * Caroline Nazareno * Tezmin Ition Tsai
Hülya N. Yılmaz * Faleeha Hassan * Jackie Davis Allen
Teresa E. Gallion * Anna Jakubczak Vel Ratty Adalan
Alicja Maria Kuberska * Shareef Abdur – Rasheed
Kimberly Burnham * Elizabeth Castillo
Nizar Sartawi * William S. Peters, Sr.
The Year of the Poet V
March 2018
Featured Poets
Iram Fatima 'Ashi'
Cassandra Swan
Jaleel Khazaal
Shazia Zaman
Mexico
Cuba
Belize
Jamaica
Haiti
Puerto Rico
Guatemala
El Salvador
Nicaragua
Costa Rica
Panama
Caribbean
&
Middle America
The Poetry Posse 2018
Gail Weston Shazor * Nizar Sartawi * Hulya N. Yılmaz
Jackie Davis Allen * Caroline 'Ceri' Nazareno
Alicja Maria Kuberska * Teresa E. Gallion
Faleeha Hassan * Shareef Abdur – Rasheed
Kimberly Burnham * Elizabeth Castillo
Tezmin Ition Tsai * William S. Peters, Sr.
The Year of the Poet V
April 2018
Featured Poets
The Nez Perce

**Now Available**

www.innerchildpress.com/the-year-of-the-poet

The Year of the Poet V
September 2018
The Aztecs & Incas
Featured Poets
The Poetry Posse 2018
The Year of the Poet V
October 2018
Featured Poets
Alicia Minjarez * Lonneice Weeks-Badley
Lopamudra Mishra * Abdelwahed Souayah
Bengali
The Poetry Posse 2018
Gail Weston Shazor * Nizar Sartawi * Hülya N. Yılmaz
Jackie Davis Allen * Caroline 'Ceri' Nazareno
Alicja Maria Kuberska * Teresa E. Gallion
Kimberly Burnham * Shareef Abdur – Rasheed
Ashok K. Bhargava * Elizabeth Castillo * Swapna Behaera
Tezmin Ition Tsai * William S. Peters, Sr.
The Year of the Poet V
November 2018
Featured Poets
Michelle Joan Barulich * Monsif Beroual
Krystyna Konecka * Nassira Nezzar
The Poetry Posse 2018
The Year of the Poet V
December 2018
Featured Poets
Rose Terranova Cirigliano
Joanna Kalinowska
Sokolović Emin
Dr. T. Ashok Chakravarthy
The Maori
Gail Weston Shazor * Nizar Sartawi * Hülya N. Yılmaz
Jackie Davis Allen * Caroline 'Ceri' Nazareno
Alicja Maria Kuberska * Teresa E. Gallion
Kimberly Burnham * Shareef Abdur – Rasheed
Ashok K. Bhargava * Elizabeth Castillo * Swapna Behera
Tezmin Ition Tsai * William S. Peters, Sr.

## Now Available

www.innerchildpress.com/the-year-of-the-poet

## Inner Child Press Anthologies

### The Year of the Poet VI
**January 2019**

Indigenous North Americans

Featured Poets

**Houda Elfchtali**
**Anthony Briscoe**
**Iram Fatima 'Ashi'**
**Dr. K. K. Mathew**

*Dream Catcher*

The Poetry Posse 2019

Gail Weston Shazor * Joe Paire * Hülya N. Yilmaz
Jackie Davis Allen * Caroline 'Ceri' Nazareno
Alicja Maria Kuberska * Teresa E. Gallion
Kimberly Burnham * Shareef Abdur – Rasheed
Ashok K. Bhargava * Elizabeth Castillo * Swapna Behera
Tezmin Ition Tsai * William S. Peters, Sr.

### The Year of the Poet VI
February 2019

Featured Poets

**Marek Lukaszewicz * Bharati Nayak**
**Aida G. Roque * Jean-Jacques Fournier**

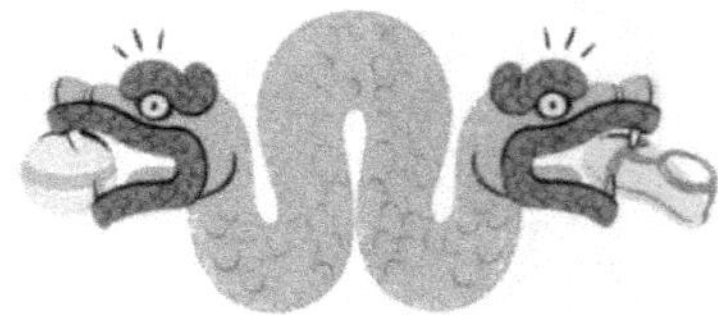

Meso-America

The Poetry Posse 2019

Gail Weston Shazor * Albert Carrasco * Hülya N. Yilmaz
Jackie Davis Allen * Caroline Nazareno * Eliza Segiet
Alicja Maria Kuberska * Teresa E. Gallion * Joe Paire
Kimberly Burnham * Shareef Abdur – Rasheed
Ashok K. Bhargava * Elizabeth Castillo * Swapna Behera
Tezmin Ition Tsai * William S. Peters, Sr.

The Year of the Poet VI
March 2019
Featured Poets
Enesa Mahmić * Sylwia K. Malinowska
Shurouk Hammoud * Anwer Ghani
The Caribbean
The Poetry Posse 2019
Gail Weston Shazor * Albert Carrasco * Hülya N. Yilmaz
Jackie Davis Allen * Caroline Nazareno * Eliza Segiet
Alicja Maria Kuberska * Teresa E. Gallion * Joe Paire
Kimberly Burnham * Shareef Abdur – Rasheed
Ashok K. Bhargava * Elizabeth Castillo * Swapna Behera
Tezmin Ition Tsai * William S. Peters, Sr.

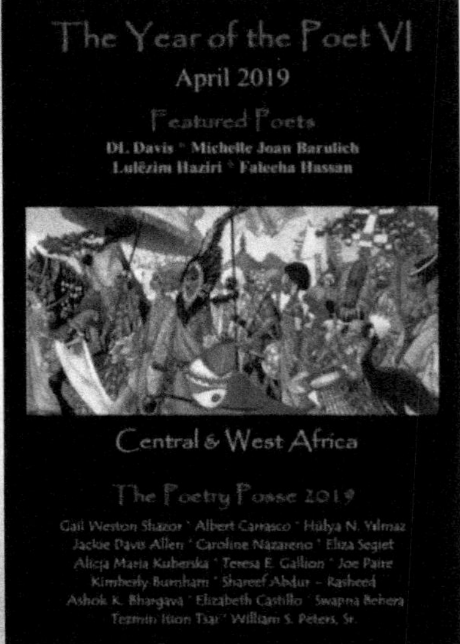
The Year of the Poet VI
April 2019
Featured Poets
DL Davis * Michelle Joan Barulich
Lulëzim Haziri * Faleeha Hassan
Central & West Africa
The Poetry Posse 2019
Gail Weston Shazor * Albert Carrasco * Hülya N. Yilmaz
Jackie Davis Allen * Caroline Nazareno * Eliza Segiet
Alicja Maria Kuberska * Teresa E. Gallion * Joe Paire
Kimberly Burnham * Shareef Abdur – Rasheed
Ashok K. Bhargava * Elizabeth Castillo * Swapna Behera
Tezmin Ition Tsai * William S. Peters, Sr.

## Now Available

www.innerchildpress.com/the-year-of-the-poet

The Year of the Poet VI
May 2019
Featured Poets
Emad Al-Haydary * Hussein Nasser Jabr
Wahab Sheriff * Abdul Razzaq Al Ameeri
Asia Southeast Asia and Maritime Asia
The Poetry Posse 2019
The Year of the Poet VI
June 2019
Featured Poets
Kate Gaudi Powiekszone * Sahaj Sabharwal
Iwu Jeff * Mohamed Abdel Aziz Shmeis
Arctic
Circumpolar
The Poetry Posse 2019
Gail Weston Shazor * Albert Carrasco * Hülya N. Yılmaz
Jackie Davis Allen * Caroline Nazareno * Eliza Segiet
Alicja Maria Kuberska * Teresa E. Gallion * Joe Paire
Kimberly Burnham * Shareef Abdur – Rasheed
Ashok K. Bhargava * Elizabeth Castillo * Swapna Behera
Tezmin Ition Tsai * William S. Peters, Sr.
The Year of the Poet VI
Featured Poets
The Horn of Africa
Ethiopia
Djibouti
Somalia
Eritrea
The Poetry Posse 2019
The Year of the Poet VI
August 2019
Featured Poets
Shola Balogun * Bharati Nayak
Monalisa Dash Dwibedy * Mbizo Chirasha
Coexist
Southwest Asia
The Poetry Posse 2019
Gail Weston Shazor * Albert Carrasco * Hülya N. Yılmaz
Jackie Davis Allen * Caroline Nazareno * Eliza Segiet
Alicja Maria Kuberska * Teresa E. Gallion * Joe Paire
Kimberly Burnham * Shareef Abdur – Rasheed
Ashok K. Bhargava * Elizabeth Castillo * Swapna Behera
Tezmin Ition Tsai * William S. Peters, Sr.

The Year of the Poet VI
September 2019
Featured Poets
Elena Liliana Popescu * Gobinda Biswas
Iram Fatima 'Ashi' * Joseph S. Spence, Sr
The Caucasus
The Poetry Posse 2019

The Year of the Poet VI
October 2019
Featured Poets
Ngozi Olivia Osuoha * Denisa Kondić
Pankhuri Sinha * Christena AV Williams
The Nile Valley
The Poetry Posse 2019

The Year of the Poet VI
November 2019
Featured Poets
Rozalia Aleksandrova * Orbindu Ganga
Smruti Ranjan Mohanty * Sofia Skleida
China
East Asia
Northern Asia
The Poetry Posse 2019

The Year of the Poet VI
December 2019
Featured Poets
Oceania
The Poetry Posse 2019

**Now Available**

www.innerchildpress.com/the-year-of-the-poet

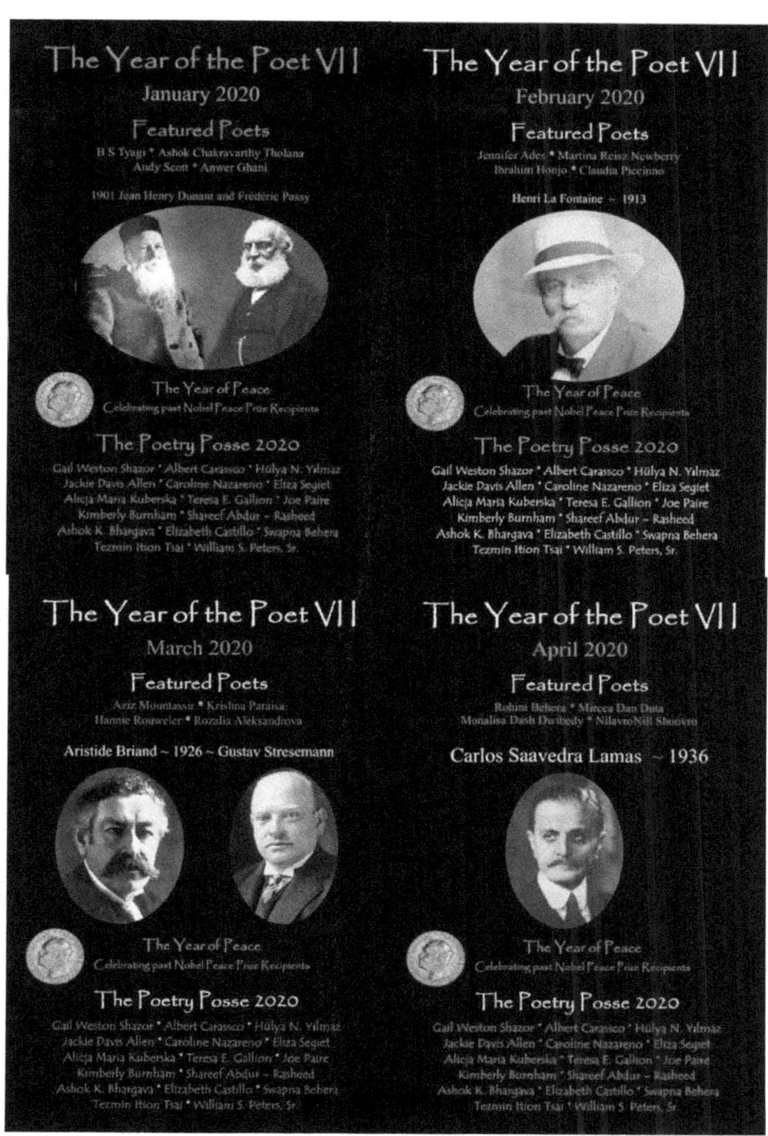
The Year of the Poet VII
January 2020
Featured Poets
1901 Jean Henry Dunant and Frédéric Passy
The Year of Peace
The Poetry Posse 2020
The Year of the Poet VII
February 2020
Featured Poets
Henri La Fontaine ~ 1913
The Year of Peace
Celebrating past Nobel Peace Prize Recipients
The Poetry Posse 2020
Gail Weston Shazor * Albert Carassco * Hülya N. Yılmaz
Jackie Davis Allen * Caroline Nazareno * Eliza Segiet
Alicja Maria Kuberska * Teresa E. Gallion * Joe Paire
Kimberly Burnham * Shareef Abdur - Rasheed
Ashok K. Bhargava * Elizabeth Castillo * Swapna Behera
Tezmin Ition Tsai * William S. Peters, Sr.
The Year of the Poet VII
March 2020
Featured Poets
Aristide Briand ~ 1926 ~ Gustav Stresemann
The Year of Peace
The Poetry Posse 2020
The Year of the Poet VII
April 2020
Featured Poets
Carlos Saavedra Lamas ~ 1936
The Year of Peace
The Poetry Posse 2020

**Now Available**

www.innerchildpress.com/the-year-of-the-poet

The Year of the Poet VII
May 2020
Featured Poets
Alok Kumar Ray * Eden S. Trinidad
Franco Barbato * Izabela Zubko
Ralph Bunche ~ 1950
The Year of Peace
Celebrating past Nobel Peace Prize Recipients
The Poetry Posse 2020
Gail Weston Shazor * Albert Carassco * Hülya N. Yılmaz
Jackie Davis Allen * Caroline Nazareno * Eliza Segiet
Alicja Maria Kuberska * Teresa E. Gallion * Joe Paire
Kimberly Burnham * Shareef Abdur – Rasheed
Ashok K. Bhargava * Elizabeth Castillo * Swapna Behera
Tezmin Ition Tsai * William S. Peters, Sr.
The Year of the Poet VII
June 2020
Featured Poets
Albert John Lutuli ~ 1960
The Year of Peace
Celebrating past Nobel Peace Prize Recipients
The Poetry Posse 2020
Gail Weston Shazor * Albert Carassco * Hülya N. Yılmaz
Jackie Davis Allen * Caroline Nazareno * Eliza Segiet
Alicja Maria Kuberska * Teresa E. Gallion * Joe Paire
Kimberly Burnham * Shareef Abdur – Rasheed
Ashok K. Bhargava * Elizabeth Castillo * Swapna Behera
Tezmin Ition Tsai * William S. Peters, Sr.
The Year of the Poet VII
July 2020
Featured Poets
Mykola Martyniuk * Orbindu Ganga
Roula Pollard * Karn Praktisha
Norman Ernest Borlaug ~ 1970
The Year of Peace
Celebrating past Nobel Peace Prize Recipients
The Poetry Posse 2020
The Year of the Poet VII
August 2020
Featured Poets
Dr Pragya Suman * Chinh Nguyen
Srinivas Vasudev * Ugwu Leonard Ifeanyi, Jr.
Adolfo Pérez Esquivel ~ 1980
The Year of Peace
Celebrating past Nobel Peace Prize Recipients
The Poetry Posse 2020
Gail Weston Shazor * Albert Carassco * Hülya N. Yılmaz
Jackie Davis Allen * Caroline Nazareno * Eliza Segiet
Alicja Maria Kuberska * Teresa E. Gallion * Joe Paire
Kimberly Burnham * Shareef Abdur – Rasheed
Ashok K. Bhargava * Elizabeth Castillo * Swapna Behera
Tezmin Ition Tsai * William S. Peters, Sr.

Now Available

www.innerchildpress.com/the-year-of-the-poet

The Year of the Poet VII
September 2020
Featured Poets
Mikhail Sergeyevich Gorbachev ~ 1990
The Year of Peace
Celebrating past Nobel Peace Prize Recipients
The Poetry Posse 2020
The Year of the Poet VII
October 2020
Featured Poets
Mutawaf A. Shaheed * Galina Italyanskaya
Nadeem Fraz * Avril Tanya Meallem
Kim Dae-jung ~ 2000
The Year of Peace
Celebrating past Nobel Peace Prize Recipients
The Poetry Posse 2020
The Year of the Poet VII
November 2020
Featured Poets
Liu Xiaobo ~ 2010
The Year of Peace
Celebrating past Nobel Peace Prize Recipients
The Poetry Posse 2020
The Year of the Poet VII
December 2020
Featured Poets
Ratan Ghosh * Ibtisam Ibrahim Al-Asady
Brindha Vinodh * Selma Kopic
Abiy Ahmed Ali ~ 2019
The Year of Peace
Celebrating past Nobel Peace Prize Recipients
The Poetry Posse 2020
Gail Weston Shazor * Albert Carassco * Hülya N. Yılmaz
Jackie Davis Allen * Caroline Nazareno * Eliza Segiet
Alicja Maria Kuberska * Teresa E. Gallion * Joe Paire
Kimberly Burnham * Shareef Abdur – Rasheed
Ashok K. Bhargava * Elizabeth Castillo * Swapna Behera
Tezmin Ition Tsai * William S. Peters, Sr.


Now Available

www.innerchildpress.com/the-year-of-the-poet

The Year of the Poet VIII
January 2021
Featured Global Poets
Andrew Scott * Debaprasanna Biswas
Shakil Kalam * Changming Yuan
Banksy's The Girl with the Pierced Eardrum
Poetry . . . Ekphrasticly Speaking
The Poetry Posse 2020
Gail Weston Shazor * Albert Carassco * Hülya N. Yılmaz
Jackie Davis Allen * Caroline Nazareno * Eliza Segiet
Alicja Maria Kuberska * Teresa E. Gallion * Joe Paire
Kimberly Burnham * Shareef Abdur – Rasheed
Ashok K. Bhargava * Elizabeth Castillo * Swapna Behera
Tezmin Ition Tsai * William S. Peters, Sr.

The Year of the Poet VIII
February 2021
Featured Global Poets
T. Ramesh Babu * Ruchida Barman
Neptune Barman * Faleeha Hassan
Emory Douglas : 1968 Olympics mural
Poetry . . . Ekphrasticly Speaking
The Poetry Posse 2021
Gail Weston Shazor * Albert Carassco * Hülya N. Yılmaz
Jackie Davis Allen * Caroline Nazareno * Eliza Segiet
Alicja Maria Kuberska * Teresa E. Gallion * Joe Paire
Kimberly Burnham * Shareef Abdur – Rasheed
Ashok K. Bhargava * Elizabeth Castillo * Swapna Behera
Tezmin Ition Tsai * William S. Peters, Sr.

The Year of the Poet VIII
March 2021
Featured Global Poets
Claudia Piccinno * Mohammed Jabr
Luzviminda Rivera *Nigar Arif
Tatyana Fazlalizadeh
Poetry . . . Ekphrasticly Speaking
The Poetry Posse 2021
Gail Weston Shazor * Albert Carassco * Hülya N. Yılmaz
Jackie Davis Allen * Caroline Nazareno * Eliza Segiet
Alicja Maria Kuberska * Teresa E. Gallion * Joe Paire
Kimberly Burnham * Shareef Abdur – Rasheed
Ashok K. Bhargava * Elizabeth Castillo * Swapna Behera
Tezmin Ition Tsai * William S. Peters, Sr.

The Year of the Poet VIII
April 2021
Featured Global Poets
Katarzyna Brus- Sawczuk * Anwesha Paul
Rozalia Aleksandrova * Shahid Abbas
Pablo O'Higgins
Poetry . . . Ekphrasticly Speaking
The Poetry Posse 2021
Gail Weston Shazor * Albert Carassco * Hülya N. Yılmaz
Jackie Davis Allen * Caroline Nazareno * Eliza Segiet
Alicja Maria Kuberska * Teresa E. Gallion * Joe Paire
Kimberly Burnham * Shareef Abdur – Rasheed
Ashok K. Bhargava * Elizabeth Castillo * Swapna Behera
Tezmin Ition Tsai * William S. Peters, Sr.

## Now Available

www.innerchildpress.com/the-year-of-the-poet

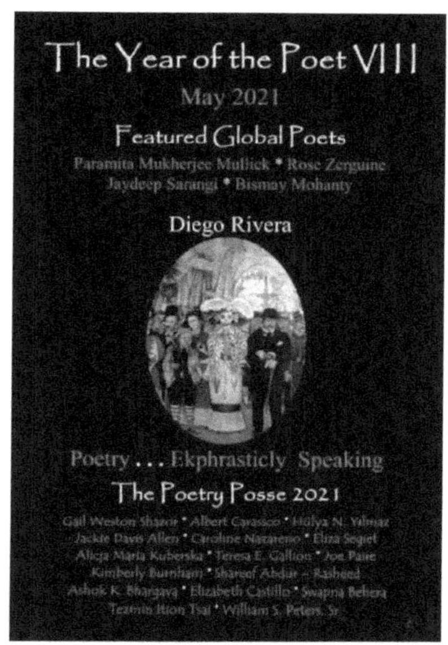
The Year of the Poet VIII
May 2021
Featured Global Poets
Paramita Mukherjee Mullick * Rose Zerguine
Jaydeep Sarangi * Bismay Mohanty
Diego Rivera
Poetry . . . Ekphrasticly Speaking
The Poetry Posse 2021

Now Available

www.innerchildpress.com/the-year-of-the-poet

and there is much, much more !

visit . . .

www.innerchildpress.com/anthologies-sales-special.php

Also check out our Authors and all the wonderful Books Available at :

www.innerchildpress.com/authors-pages

INNER CHILD PRESS
WORLD HEALING
WORLD PEACE
2018
A Poetry Anthology for Humanity

*Now Available*

www.worldhealingworldpeacepoetry.com

i support
World Healing
World Peace

www.worldhealingworldpeacepoetry.com

World Healing World Peace
PoEtRy
i am a believer!

# World Healing World Peace

2012, 2014, 2016, 2018, 2020

*Now Available*

www.worldhealingworldpeacepoetry.com

# Inner Child Press International

*'building bridges of cultural understanding'*

## Meet the Board of Directors

William S. Peters, Sr.
Chair Person
Founder
Inner Child Enterprises
Inner Child Press

Hülya N Yilmaz
Director
Editing Services
Co-Chair Person

Fahredin B. Shehu
Director
Cultural Affairs

Elizabeth E. Castillo
Director
Recording Secretary

De'Andre Hawthorne
Director
Performance Poetry

Gail Weston Shazor
Director
Anthologies

Kimberly Burnham
Director
Cultural Ambassador
Pacific Northwest
USA

Ashok K. Bhargava
Director
WINAwards

Deborah Smart
Director
Publicity
Marketing

www.innerchildpress.com

# Inner Child Press International

*'building bridges of cultural understanding'*

## Meet our Cultural Ambassadors

**Fahredin Shehu**
Director of Cultural

**Faleha Hassan**
Iraq – USA

**Elizabeth E. Castillo**
Philippines

**Antoinette Coleman**
Chicago
Midwest USA

**Ananda Nepali**
Nepal – Tibet
Northern India

**Kimberly Burnham**
Pacific Northwest
USA

**Alicja Kuberska**
Poland
Eastern Europe

**Swapna Behera**
India
Southeast Asia

**Kolade O. Freedom**
Nigeria
West Africa

**Monsif Beroual**
Morocco
Northern Africa

**Ashok K. Bhargava**
Canada

**Tzemin Ition Tsai**
Republic of China
Greater China

**Alicia M. Ramirez**
Mexico
Central America

**Christena AV Williams**
Jamaica
Caribbean

**Louise Hudon**
Eastern Canada

**Aziz Mountassir**
Morocco
Northern Africa

**Shareef Abdur-Rasheed**
Southeastern USA

**Laure Charazac**
France
Western Europe

**Mohammad Ikbal Harb**
Lebanon
Middle East

**Mohamed Abdel Aziz Shmeis**
Egypt
Middle East

**Hillary Mainga**
Kenya
Eastern Africa

**Josephus R. Johnson**
Liberia

www.innerchildpress.com

This Anthological Publication
is underwritten solely by

## Inner Child Press International

Inner Child Press is a Publishing Company Founded and Operated by Writers. Our personal publishing experiences provides us an intimate understanding of the sometimes daunting challenges Writers, New and Seasoned may face in the Business of Publishing and Marketing their Creative "Written Work".

For more Information

Inner Child Press International

www.innerchildpress.com

Inner Child Press International

'building bridges of cultural understanding'

202 Wiltree Court, State College, Pennsylvania 16801

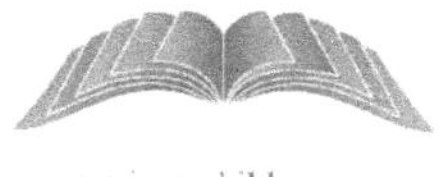

www.innerchildpress.com

~ fini ~

www.ingramcontent.com/pod-product-compliance
Lightning Source LLC
LaVergne TN
LVHW051045080426
835508LV00019B/1714

* 9 7 8 1 9 5 2 0 8 1 5 0 7 *